LILY OF THE MOHAWKS

Lily
of the
Mohawks

THE STORY OF
St. Kateri

EMILY CAVINS

SERVANT
BOOKS

PUBLISHED BY FRANCISCAN MEDIA
Cincinnati, Ohio

Cover and book design by Mark Sullivan
Cover image © Kevin Gordon | kevingordonportraits.com

LIBRARY OF CONGRESS CATALOGING-IN-PUBLICATION DATA
Cavins, Emily.
Lily of the Mohawks : the story of St. Kateri / Emily Cavins.
pages cm
Summary: "Even before Kateri Tekakwitha's canonization on October 21, 2012, many had been inspired by the story of the young Native American mystic who lived in the Mohawk Valley during the seventeenth century. With Emily Cavins's skill for weaving together historical facts and a compelling story, readers will discover Kateri's path to sainthood against the backdrop of her life as a Native American in New York. These pages will reveal: What led to Kateri's desire to become a Christian . Her piety and self-denial in the face of persecution and illness. Her impact on the Catholic Mohawk community The long road to sainthood, including two miracles attributed to Kateri More than just a compelling story of Kateri's short life, readers will also learn how to avail themselves of Kateri's intercession, why Kateri has become known as the patron saint of the environment, and of her connection to St. Francis of Assisi"— Provided by publisher.
ISBN 978-1-61636-555-4 (pbk.)
1. Tekakwitha, Kateri, Saint, 1656-1680. 2. Mohawk women—Biography. 3. Christian saints—New York (State)—Biography. 4. Mohawk Indians—Religion. I. Title.
E99.M8T4567 2013
282.092—dc23
[B]
2013025737

ISBN 978-1-61636-555-4

Published by Servant Books, an imprint of Franciscan Media
28 W. Liberty St.
Cincinnati, OH 45202
www.FranciscanMedia.org

Printed in the United States of America.
Printed on acid-free paper.
13 14 15 16 17 5 4 3 2 1

This book is dedicated to my daughters,
Carly, Jaki, and Toni,
and my goddaughters,
Hannah and Mary.

Contents

Acknowledgments

I first would like to acknowledge the Jesuits for their passion for missions and for carefully recording their work in New France. St. Kateri is the fruit of their labor.

Thanks for the willingness of Dr. Dean Snow of Penn State University in sharing with me his expertise on the Iroquois. He led the Mohawk Valley archaeological excavations in the 1980s and was involved in cataloging the items from the St. Kateri Shrine when it was turned over to the New York State Museum. I had the delight of traveling with my dear friend, Jeannie Burkhead, to the land of St. Kateri while researching this book. Her companionship was invaluable. I want to thank Claudia Volkman who encouraged me to take the plunge to write about St. Kateri. Thanks to Sr. Kateri Mitchell, the executive director of the Tekakwitha Conference for her insights. I'm grateful for Ann Brown from New Hope Publications, Fr. Steven Hoffman, Fr. Michael Skluzacek, Br. John Paul, Sr. Marie Rose Messingschlager, C.D.P., Jean McGinty, Tom Porter, Deacon Richard Wright, and the staff members at the shrines in New York. Of course, my husband Jeff, who endured the hours of writing, was my greatest supporter.

Over the past hundred years the attitude to Native Americans has radically changed. From the time Europeans arrived in America, the common approach was a general dismissal of "Indians" as enemies from an inferior culture who stood in the way of expansion and progress. At times they were recruited as allies against the French colonists in Canada, but then were discarded when they were no longer useful. Well into the twentieth century, such images were associated with unscrupulous purveyors of guns and whiskey who caused trouble between the Indians and white settlers for their own selfish reasons. However, the ever-victorious settlers and soldiers in the Indian Wars, especially in the West, dominated the impression of Native Americans in books and movies.

By the late twentieth century, a more sympathetic attitude toward Native Americans developed, not only in terms of greater awareness of the federal government's many broken treaties with the tribes but also revelations of the terrible conditions that existed on federally run reservations. This new awareness and sympathy frequently led to a fascination with Native American religions. Sometimes the interest fit into the 1960s counterculture, as when Carlos Castaneda wrote about the use of the drug peyote and the Native American religion in his *Teachings of Don Juan: A Yaqui Way of Knowledge*. Other times Native American religious practices, such as sweat lodges, drumming, and the burning of sweet grass, were incorporated by folks ranging from New

Age followers to various Catholic groups who wanted to inculturate Native American traditions and learn from them. Unfortunately some of these attempts showed little appreciation for the distinctive religions and practices of the highly diverse Native American religions and cultures by mixing and matching Lakota Sioux, Hopi, and other nations together.

As this appreciation of Native American culture, religion, and history developed, many others developed an antipathy to the Christian missionaries who sought to introduce the Indian nations to Jesus Christ. Generally, the missionaries were seen simply as extensions of the colonial powers who wanted to conquer, enslave, or exterminate the native peoples of the Americas. In reality, the history of the missionaries is quite mixed. Shamefully, some did serve to expand the colonial powers. Others stood up against colonists and defended the Native Americans from enslavement, degradation, and extermination. Some also gave their lives in order to spread faith in Jesus Christ, either at the hands of the Native Americans or at the hands of fellow European colonists. Most of them loved the Native Americans to whom they went with the Gospel of Christ. In fact it was the Jesuit missionaries who wrote the seventy-three–volume *The Jesuit Relations* and many other missionaries who preserved the native languages in dictionaries and grammars and described the customs and practices of the various tribes. Modern Native Americans often go back to these sources in order to recover elements of their ancestors' cultures, and they frequently have come to appreciate the love that the missionaries had for their peoples.

The story of St. Kateri Tekakwitha shows the effects of that love on her and other native people. The missionaries did not seek to spread a European culture but to bring Christ into an existing native culture. The effect of Christian faith on St. Kateri gave her a realization of the dignity she had within herself. This recognition of her dignity was the occasion for a decision to grow in holiness. Instead of destroying her culture, her faith raised it to a new level that led her closer to Jesus Christ.

St. Kateri is the second Native American saint, after Juan Diego of Mexico. Other great Native American Catholics include Black Elk, a committed catechist among the Sioux, and Chief Seattle of the Duwamish. They are welcomed in heaven by the holy priests who went before them, such as the North American Martyrs and Blessed Junipero Serra. Together they worship God in heaven and pray for the rest of us here on earth. May this study of St. Kateri help us all to seek an authentic holiness that elevates us and our culture by the graces Jesus Christ our Savior bestows on each of us as he did on her.

—Fr. Mitch Pacwa, S.J.

In the host of saints of the Catholic Church, there has never been one so connected to the earth, yet so joined to the Spirit. The rhythm of the seasons, the cycles of the moon, the bounty of the harvests, and the elements of wind and fire surrounded her each day. And from this organic simplicity, a huge capacity for spiritual communion with Christ was nurtured and matured like a mighty tree, the symbol of the Iroquois. Yet St. Kateri Tekakwitha remained a gentle lily.

A Native American from the Iroquois League, St. Kateri has aptly come to be known as Lily of the Mohawks. Her purity of soul resonates with anyone who learns about her life of hardship during a period of history like no other. Though her life was simple, her depth and spirituality show just why this woman has become a beloved saint.

St. Kateri was born in a small village of the Mohawks to a Christian Algonquin mother and a Mohawk chief. When she was four years old, her parents died of smallpox, while she survived the disease with permanent scars. Baptized at the age of twenty when Jesuit missionaries came to her village, she later moved to a mission in Canada, where she received her first Communion and took a vow of virginity. She died at the age of twenty-four from ill health.

So, what does this simple synopsis fail to reveal to us about the person of St. Kateri Tekakwitha? At her core was an unwavering faith in Jesus Christ—an active faith that enveloped her from the moment she first heard the Gospel until the day of her death; a lively faith, demonstrated through many acts of devotion to Christ and a kindness toward others.

We know about St. Kateri through the writings of several Jesuit fathers, some who observed her life as a Christian and others who recorded the events of their own missionary efforts in the New World. We know about her environment through the writings of early Europeans who had contact with the Mohawks, archaeological surveys of Mohawk sites in present day New York state, and our understanding of the traditions of the Iroquois lifestyle of the seventeenth century, in the context of the political turmoil during her lifetime. Three hundred fifty years have passed since St. Kateri's death, and hundreds of books have been written about her and the Iroquois. It is upon the shoulders of those who have documented the historical time period and her life that we can view a more complete picture of just who she was.

Amid the academic facts and dates of her life, we can explore the amazing nature of her spiritual journey toward sainthood. And with a better understanding of who she is, we can be proud to claim her as the first Native American saint from North America—someone we can confidently approach with our requests for her gracious intercession.

What's in a Name?

There are several variations on the spelling and pronunciation of St. Kateri's name, but in this book, we will use the spelling of Kateri Tekakwitha. "Kateri" is the Iroquois pronunciation of her baptismal name, which means Catherine, after St. Catherine of Siena. Though Catherine was a common baptismal name at the time, the lives of St. Kateri and St. Catherine of Siena also enjoyed several key similarities, including a lifestyle of asceticism, a vow of virginity, and a young death.

"Tekakwitha" is her Iroquois name, which the Jesuit fathers also called her. In the Iroquois tradition, babies were formally named at particular seasons of the year during traditional ceremonies. A tradition has arisen in later centuries that her name was "Little Sunshine" as a baby, but in early accounts of her life this name was not mentioned. She became known as Tekakwitha after she was adopted by her uncle when she was almost five. It was not uncommon for an Iroquois to change names several times during his or her lifetime. Because Tekakwitha had difficulty seeing in the aftermath of smallpox affliction, her name most likely meant "One Who Bumps Into Things."[1] She received the name Catherine at her baptism at the age of twenty. In this book, she will be referred to as Tekakwitha before her baptism and Kateri after her baptism.

St. Kateri has been identified as the "Lily of the Mohawks," which was based on a phrase written by Fr. Claude Chauchetiere in his biography of her life.[2] He called her a "lily among thorns," in reference to the difficulty of living a Christian life in the midst of a traditional Mohawk tribe. Thus, illustrations often depict her with lilies—which are also associated with purity, for which St. Kateri is known due to her vow of perpetual virginity.

. . . .

Author's Note: Fact or Fiction?
There are many entertaining accounts of the life of St. Kateri that do not distinguish between fact and fiction. In this book, I have only included facts that can be substantiated in written form from the accounts of the Jesuits or related sources—qualifying my personal interpretations with a "perhaps" or a "may have." This account is based on up-to-date research, as well as recorded accounts from the seventeenth century.

As you will see, the facts of St. Kateri's life that are available to us will show her worthiness of sainthood without any need for embellishment of my own.

St. Kateri, pray for us. May your powerful journey of faith inspire us all.
. . . .

TEKAKWITHA'S NATIVE HERITAGE

Tekakwitha belonged to the strongest Native American nation in all of North America: the Iroquois. As she grew, her people experienced a dramatic metamorphosis, caused in large part by the mixing of cultures and religious practices. This element of change paints the backdrop for the story of Tekakwitha.

In the mid-seventeenth century, the Iroquois completely dominated the area in what is today the northeast United States—and were capable of defending their territory from any rival Native American tribe. The Iroquois League was a union of five tribes that included the Oneida, Onondaga, Cayuga, Seneca, and Mohawk—Tekakwitha's tribe.

In the region, the Mohawk were stationed furthest to the east, bordering the Hudson River on the east and the St. Lawrence on the north. To the west of the Mohawk were the Oneida. In the center were the Onondaga, with the Cayuga and then the Seneca furthest to the west, just below Lake Ontario.

This Five Nation League, the Iroquois, referred to themselves as "The People of the Longhouse" after their dwellings. A longhouse was an elm bark structure, often one hundred feet in length, that could house up to 150 people.[3] The Iroquois way of life revolved around the longhouse, which not only served as shelter but hosted many ceremonies and festivals. An Iroquois village was made up of several longhouses built close together.

Each longhouse within a village was the home for one extended family, with smaller nuclear family units—related to the clan mother of the longhouse—stationed along the length of it on either side of a central aisle. In the Iroquois matrilineal culture, a man moved into the home of the woman after they married, and their children were traced through their mother's lineage.

The term "Iroquois" is a French rendition of a derogatory Algonquin term meaning "The Killer People"—an apt description of the Iroquois among surrounding Native American tribes. The term "Mohawk"— meaning "Man-eaters" due to the Mohawk's practice of eating their enemies on occasion—is also a term used by other Native American tribes to describe them. The Mohawks called themselves *Kanien'gehaga*, once translated as "The People of the Flint" but more recently believed to mean "The People of the Diamonds." Within the Mohawk Valley, there still can be found quartz crystals, now called Herkimer diamonds, which were used as amulets and trade items until glass beads came upon the scene through trade with the Europeans.

Women in the Iroquois League played a central role in their society, not only in domestic food preparation, farming, and child rearing, but also in the most important decisions facing the tribe. They were the ones who chose the chiefs and decided when it was time to go to war. They were also in charge of arranging marriages. The Iroquois were divided into clans within each tribe, and a spouse had to be chosen from a clan other than one's own.

It is reported by the Jesuits that Tekakwitha was of the Turtle Clan, which was the clan of her father. In traditional circumstances, a child would be of the mother's clan, but as a captive from the Algonquin tribe, Tekakwitha's mother would have carried the name of the clan who adopted her.[4] When an Iroquois reached puberty, he or she was then given a clan name which had once belonged to a deceased member of the clan, so in a sense the deceased was brought back into the clan. We do not know if Tekakwitha was a clan name or not.

The clan system among the Iroquois acted like the skeletal system of the body holding the society together. The division into clans was crucial in decision making within the tribe and within the league because it kept the clans accountable to one another. A main function of clans was to assist one another during times of grief: one clan would carry on daily chores for the clan that was suffering a loss. Of the three Mohawk clans, Turtle, Bear, and Wolf, the Turtle was the main clan. Even today, modern Mohawks attribute the characteristics of the steady turtle to their personalities and a close identity to one's clan is still prevalent.[5]

BIRTH OF THE IROQUOIS LEAGUE

The story of the founding of the Iroquois League describes how Hiawatha and the Peacekeeper brought the five tribes together at the council fire in Onondaga territory near what is today Syracuse, New York. Wampum beads—made from clamshells of purple or white—were strung together as a sign of their agreement, and the five tribes stopped warring with one another and formed the strongest grouping of tribes in the Northeast. The League began to govern the tribes through the civil chiefs, who were clan leaders from each of the Iroquois villages. The chiefs would convene at the great council fire in Onondaga territory to discuss issues and make decisions through a process of checks and balances among the clans. Tekakwitha's father was most likely this type of chief.

The council would begin with prayer to the Creator and end with a recitation of "The Words that Come Before All Else," an address of thanksgiving for the natural world. The Iroquois would also recite the Great Law of Peace, which included all types of laws, from festival observance and treatment of others to matters of war.

Each nation had a set number of chiefs to sit at the council, with the Onondaga having the most at fourteen and the Seneca the fewest at eight. In addition to the clan chiefs, in each tribe there were also war chiefs, who led the warriors during fighting and raiding.

In order to summon the chiefs to the great council fire, a messenger would deliver a string of wampum beads to each village where the chiefs resided. On the string of wampum would be a notched stick that indicated how many days until the council convened. The messenger would recite the reason for meeting at the council fire and hand the string to the intended receiver. To signify an acceptance of the message, the receiver would recite the reason back, while holding the wampum string. In the Great Law of Peace, it is described in this manner: "Any of the people of the Five Nations may use shells (or wampum) as the record of a pledge, contract or an agreement entered into and the same shall be binding as soon as shell strings shall have been exchanged by both parties" (Article 23).

In addition to strings of wampum, belts of wampum were used as contracts. The wampum belt that best symbolizes the Iroquois League is known as the Hiawatha Belt. It shows two squares on each side of a tree made of white wampum, with a background of purple wampum. These belts are considered sacred by the Iroquois and are highly treasured to this day. The five shapes symbolize the five nations that came together to form the Iroquois League, most likely in 1536, based on the date of a solar eclipse mentioned in their oral tradition.[6]

The villages of the Mohawks were often built along the bluffs overlooking the Mohawk River, which flowed into the Hudson. Pine forests abounding in wildlife spread across their territory on both sides of the river, and elm and maple trees also grew in abundance. In this setting, the Mohawks dwelled in a society rich in traditions, thriving on the ingenuity of their elders, the strength of their warriors, and the industriousness of their women.

Drying methods of food storage kept them supplied through the winter with an abundance of corn, dried berries, herbs, and mushrooms, as well as smoked meat and fish. Fresh meat from bear and deer strengthened them all year long—and every part of the animals they killed was used. Muscle sinew became strong thread to bind bark in place on their longhouses. Bear grease became a skin lotion and was also used to soften buckskin processed into clothing and moccasins. Bones became tools or decorative combs or amulets. Fur pelts became blankets and clothing.

CHANGING TIMES

A Mohawk trait that Tekakwitha exhibited throughout her lifetime was resilience—part of the very fabric of the Iroquois, who had to learn to adapt to some monumental challenges. Times were changing, and the Iroquois lifestyle and traditions would be put to the test.

The first huge challenge was one of pure survival—trying to rebound from epidemics such as smallpox, which were brought about by contact with Europeans. Outbreaks of smallpox and other epidemics killed upwards of 50 percent of the Iroquois population. To counteract the population loss, however, the Iroquois raided other Native American and European settlements, capturing hundreds of people and assimilating them into their way of life. Partly in an attempt to bolster their population and partly to ensure trading channels, the Iroquois, with the Mohawks leading the way, dominated the Northeast with raiding parties, eventually driving out or assimilating the Huron, Algonquin, and dozens of other tribes, from New England to Lake Superior.

Ready trade would only intensify these warlike tendencies of the Iroquois. The Dutch began to settle near the Mohawks in 1624 after the West India Company set up the trading post of Fort Orange on the eastern edge of Mohawk territory along the Hudson River—near modern-day Albany. The Dutch made claim to the Hudson area after Henry Hudson made an expedition up the river from Manhattan, and the relationship between the Dutch and the Iroquois was very congenial. The Iroquois quickly supplied the Dutch with furs in exchange for items they had never encountered before, such as firearms, which they became adept at using. This helped the Mohawks to gain the upper hand over other tribes who were armed with only traditional bows and arrows, maces, tomahawks, and spears. Every non-Iroquois dreaded an ambush by these fierce and effective warriors.

Trade with Europeans would, however, create an unforeseen challenge for the Iroquois and Native Americans in general: the introduction of alcohol. Just as the Native Americans had no immunity to European epidemics, they had no resistance to alcohol. Whiskey from the Dutch introduced drunken binges to Iroquois villages that left them in a stupor for days. Traditionally, the Iroquois were known as great orators and negotiators, but when they were under the influence of alcohol, it was easy to take advantage of them and have them sign away their territory.

Finally, the erosion of the traditional respect for nature began to occur at this time as well, due to the demand for furs. The beaver was killed nearly to extinction in some areas. This depletion of natural resources was uncharacteristic of Native Americans, who traditionally only killed what they needed for themselves. When an animal was killed, the Iroquois would offer a prayer of thanksgiving to the Creator for the animal and also thanked the animal for its gift of itself. The killing of animals for profit was a new concept among the tribes of the region.

As these and many other factors came into play, change was inevitable—but what kind? For the Mohawk tribe, the changes brought deep divisions that caused families to split apart, and Tekakwitha was caught in the middle of this widening divide.

The Iroquois had delayed the westward expansion of European settlers into their territory, but in the end, their challenges proved to be too much, as they were driven from their own homeland—along with the rest of the Native American tribes—by the governments of the United States and Canada.

There are several reservations in Canada where many Iroquois reside today, maintaining their clan system and governing themselves in councils led by chiefs, reciting their prayers in their native tongues, producing traditional items, eating traditional foods, and celebrating their native festivals. Tekakwitha would recognize their way of life in a moment—and surely does as their intercessor in heaven. Her identification with the Native Americans is one reason why the sainthood of St. Kateri is so important.

Chapter One

THE JESUITS BRING THE GOSPEL TO THE IROQUOIS
1625–1656

In the short timespan of Kateri Tekakwitha's life, the power of several empires shifted: The Iroquois, the Dutch, the British, the French, and the Kingdom of God all collided. This time period was like a shifting kaleidoscope, with cultures, religions, politics, and territories spinning around to create an ever-changing landscape of people and power.

During the volatile era of mid–seventeenth-century North America, the life of St. Kateri was one shining bead in this shifting kaleidoscope. Her life was profoundly influenced by European contact, even as she lived a simple life among the Mohawk people.

The conversion of Tekakwitha was not an isolated outpouring of the Holy Spirit onto a young woman in the wilderness. She is a testament, ultimately, to the limitless love of God—but also to the blood of the martyrs and the prayers of her holy mother. She lived in a culture whose customs and traditions stretched back many centuries, but the spread of the Gospel during the seventeenth century added a new dimension to the beliefs and practices of many indigenous North Americans.

Though our modern world bombards us with so many distractions, hurling us onward at a relentless pace, if we pause to observe St. Kateri Tekakwitha, we find a model of a person who was engulfed in cataclysmic change, yet exhibited simplicity, humility, and devotion to Christ. Her focus on the importance of the kingdom of God can help guide us to a place of intimacy with Christ in the midst of our world of change and uncertainty.

To help us understand how it is that those not exposed to the Gospel are led to faith, the Catholic Church teaches us that eternal life can be obtained by those who sincerely seek God and act to do his will even if they have never heard the Gospel.[1] One could imagine that the longing of many Native American hearts to know God fully was fulfilled when Jesuit missionaries, fearlessly facing unknown peril and death, brought the Gospel to North America at the prompting of the Holy Spirit.

Tekakwitha's grandparents, whom she never knew, would have been such people, longing to know God. They would have been among the first to receive the Gospel from the Jesuits, presenting their infant daughter for baptism at the rustic mission chapel of the Conception of Mary Immaculate at Three Rivers.[2] In this humble way, they helped to spread the Gospel to the whole world, by initiating the path to sainthood for their granddaughter, Tekakwitha.[3]

JESUIT MISSION AND MARTYRDOM

An instrumental factor of change for the Iroquois, the French began settling in New France, which is Canada today, and established Quebec in 1608 and Three Rivers in 1634 during the reign of Louis XIII. Samuel de Champlain explored and mapped the area of the St. Lawrence River and the Great Lakes, becoming friends with the Huron, Algonquin, and Montagnais tribes, all of which were northern enemies of the Iroquois.

In 1609, an incident occurred that solidified the enmity between the Iroquois and the French, as well as contributed to the Iroquois's attack on the French's allies, the Huron and Algonquin tribes. The Iroquois encountered Champlain and a small group of his Native American allies, and battle lines were drawn for the following day. At the beginning of the fight, Champlain used his gun to shoot two Iroquois chiefs with one shot, a phenomenon that set the Iroquois to flight in bewilderment, having never seen firearms before. From this point on, the Iroquois not only saw the French as their enemy, but also sought out and learned how to use firearms to their great advantage.

Despite the growing conflict in the region, the arrival of the French and the creation of small settlements opened the doors to French religious orders to come and minister to the settlers and do mission work among their Native American allies.

In this way, the Jesuits decided to venture to the New World, inspired by the missionary zeal of fellow Jesuit, St. Francis Xavier, who spent many years in India spreading the Gospel. Other Jesuits had followed suit, courageously proclaiming the Gospel in other faraway lands such as China, Japan, the Philippines, and South America.

The Jesuits are members of The Society of Jesus, which was founded by St. Ignatius of Loyola in 1534. He and seven companions dedicated themselves to the vows of poverty, chastity, and service to the Holy Father. In a matter of years, they had founded a network of colleges in Europe and beyond. The Jesuits were highly educated priests, filled with passion for the faith and courage to face anything. A handful of passionate French Jesuits traveled to the wilderness of New France, setting up missions along the St. Lawrence River in the territories of the Huron and Algonquin tribes.

The Jesuit style of conversion was based on enculturation. Rather than radically changing the way of life for the Native Americans, they instead incorporated into their expression of faith the Native American traditions that were compatible with Christianity. They would only forbid practices that were incongruent with Christianity, mainly cannibalism, torture, promiscuity, and sorcery. The Native Americans were

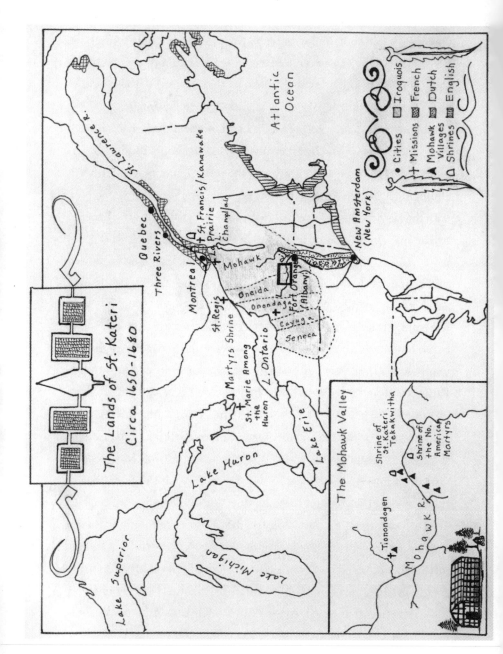

spiritual in nature and could easily understand the concept of super-natural beings and forces beyond themselves, so it was not difficult for them to grasp an array of concepts at the core of Catholic teaching—concepts such as repentance, confession, penance, meditation, respect of nature, sacrifice, offerings of thanks, and gratitude.

Although the Jesuits learned to communicate in several of the native languages, they still had difficulty explaining the Gospel to the natives, so their most effective form of communication was through drawing and painting. They illustrated Bible scenes on birch bark, helping the Native Americans to understand the spiritual message within the art especially when a theological explanation was beyond their comprehension.

Though the Jesuits had made many converts of the Huron and Algonquin tribes by the time of Tekakwitha's birth, their influence on the Mohawks had barely begun; there were no converts among them. It was quite unexpected how the Jesuits first reached the interior of Mohawk territory. The Jesuits did not come as welcomed missionaries, but rather as captives slated for torture.

In 1642, a group of Huron and French, including Fr. Isaac Jogues, were traveling by canoe along the St. Lawrence River from Three Rivers carrying supplies for the remote mission of St. Marie Among the Hurons many miles to the west. At this time, Tekakwitha's mother was a pre-teen who may have been aware of their departure from Three Rivers. She most likely would have attended a school or at least received instructions from the Jesuits stationed at Three Rivers. She may have watched as the birch bark canoes capable of carrying nearly two thousand pounds of supplies glided into the river. Perhaps after a solemn prayer for safety from those who lived at the mission, she watched the missionaries paddle away until they were only small dots on the horizon. There was always an underlying fear that a band of war-painted Mohawks would ambush those who dared leave their town walls.

On the second day of this journey, while camping near the edge of Mohawk territory, the group was attacked by a band of seventy feathered Mohawks whose horrifying whoops filled the party with dread. Swiftly, twelve elm bark canoes docked on the bank near their camp, and the Mohawk warriors descended upon them. Though the Frenchmen fought back with guns, the Mohawks prevailed, and Fr. Jogues, two other Frenchmen, and several Huron Christians were taken as prisoners.

In the fortnight of travel from their place of capture to the Mohawk village of Ossernenon,[4] the captives had their fingernails torn off and fingers mangled by warriors chewing on their exposed nail beds until they were crushed. They also endured intense beatings. When they finally reached the village, a gauntlet of young men with clubs lined up along the steep hill to the gate.

Already weak from lack of food, torture, and fear, the nearly naked prisoners were clubbed as they struggled up the hill toward a torture platform. The fainting and staggering prisoners were tied onto the platform to endure more blows, slashes from sharp shells, and burns from hot cinders. Children entered into these torture practices as well, satisfied to hear the prisoners cry out in pain. Most of the Huron captives were put to death in the process, but the Frenchmen were kept alive and eventually made slaves to families in the village of Ossernenon.

The two other Frenchmen captured with Fr. Jogues were René Goupil, a young man trained in medicine, and Guillaume Couture, who was later separated from Fr. Jogues and René to become a slave in another Mohawk village. The group of captives was brought to the other four Mohawk villages nearby to be tortured over and over again by those in neighboring towns.

The account of the sustained torture of Fr. Jogues and René is difficult to read in *The Jesuit Relations*, vol. 31. The barbarity of the torture and the unendurable pain they suffered is beyond belief. But more remarkable than the severity of the torture are the courageous spirit and actions of Fr. Jogues. When he had the chance, he comforted the Huron captives by baptizing them, hearing their confessions, and encouraging them. When his thumb was severed and thrown to the torture platform, he picked it up and exclaimed, "I offer this to you, O my God! Remembering the sacrifices that I had presented to you for seven years past, upon the Altars of your Church, I accepted this torture as a loving vengeance for the want of love and respect that I had shown, concerning your Holy Body; you heard the cries of my soul."[5] His amazing fortitude and sacrifice for the salvation of those who tortured him sowed the seeds for the salvation of the Mohawk maiden, Tekakwitha, from this very village not yet born.

Fr. Jogues and René began to heal from their tortures and worked as slaves in the village, though Fr. Jogues's hands were permanently crippled from the ordeal. He was owned by a benevolent woman who did not treat him cruelly and allowed him some amount of freedom. He and René were able to pray together outside the village, and René was even so bold as to teach children how to make the sign of the cross. This action, however, enraged the grandfather of one of the children, for the sign of the cross was highly suspected by the Mohawks of bringing disease and evil to them.

The grandfather decided this must end, so one day while they were outside the village, perhaps gathering firewood, René and Fr. Jogues were met by one of the child's relatives, who struck René in the head with a hatchet, killing him as he called out the name of Jesus. René's body was thrown into a stream and washed away before Fr. Jogues could retrieve it for proper burial. Several months later his body was found, and Fr. Jogues took the bones and hid them in a hollow tree.[6]

After several months, his owner brought Fr. Jogues with him on a fishing expedition. As they neared the Dutch town of Fort Orange, where the Mohawk River flows into the Hudson, she allowed him to escape. He made his way back to France through many other perilous adventures.

It may be hard to believe, but Fr. Jogues wanted to return to the Mohawks, minister to the Christian captives, and begin a mission where Mass could be celebrated and converts could pray together. He received a dispensation from Pope Urban to celebrate Mass using his disfigured hands that could not elevate the host.

In 1646, the opportunity arose for him and a companion, John Lalande, to return to Iroquois territory after negotiations between the French and the Iroquois led to the release of captives in exchange for peace. As part of this new treaty, Fr. Jogues headed for Mohawk territory to represent the French since he could speak the Iroquois language well. He also intended to set up a mission among the very people who had tortured him four years earlier. He felt a destiny upon himself to complete his martyrdom among those who had already abused him. His companion understood the extreme peril of their endeavor.

Fr. Jogues had left a box of clothing and his Mass kit in the village of Ossernenon during the negotiations, but when a blight hit the corn crop, a faction of the villagers blamed the problem on the strange box of Fr. Jogues. In fear of the box, they had thrown it into the river. So upon the day that Fr. Jogues and John Lalande arrived at Ossernenon, they were immediately stripped naked, beaten, and threatened with death in the morning.

In the evening, Fr. Jogues was called to dinner in the longhouse of the Bear Clan. According to a letter written to the French by the Dutch, the Turtle and Wolf Clans were not in agreement to kill Fr. Jogues, but as he entered the door of the longhouse, he was immediately struck with a hatchet and then beheaded. John Lalande met the same fate the following morning. As was customary, the heads of the defeated were placed on display upon the posts of the palisade wall that surrounded the village, and their bodies were thrown into the river.

Between the years of 1642 and 1649, eight men were martyred. These men are known as the North American Martyrs.

St. René Goupil (1642)—Jesuit brother killed by a hatchet blow to the head by a Mohawk in Ossernenon.

St. Isaac Jogues (1646)—Jesuit priest killed by a hatchet blow to the head, then beheaded by a Mohawk in Ossernenon.

St. John Lalande (1646)—Jesuit companion killed by a hatchet blow to the head, then beheaded by a Mohawk in Ossernenon.

St. Antoine Daniel (1648)—Jesuit priest shot by a Mohawk during a raid on a Huron village in Ontario. His body was burned in the church.

St. Jean de Brebeuf (1649)—Jesuit priest captured by the Iroquois from Huron mission in Ontario and tortured to death, his heart cut out, and his blood drunk by the Iroquois.

St. Gabriel Lalemant (1649)—Jesuit priest captured by the Iroquois from Huron mission in Ontario and tortured to death.

St. Noel Chabanel (1649)—Jesuit priest ambushed by a Huron while on his way to preach at a Huron village near Quebec.

St. Charles Garnier (1649)—Jesuit priest attacked by Iroquois at St. Jean Mission near Quebec who was shot and tomahawked.

Even in this milieu of distrust and confusion, the Jesuits risked their lives to bring the Gospel of Christ to the Native Americans. They carefully recorded their efforts in books and letters now called *The Jesuit Relations and Allied Documents*,[7] which powerfully reveal the fervor and dedication of many priests and their supporting staff.

TEKAKWITHA'S PARENTS

The village where the martyrdom of St. Isaac Jogues and St. René Goupil occurred was also the village of Tekakwitha's father. He most likely would have been a teen at the time they had been captured, and he would have participated in their torture. He also would have observed their conduct in the village while they were slaves and may have respected their stamina and courage, as the ability to withstand torture without crying out was highly admired among the Iroquois.

Though Tekakwitha's father was a member of the Turtle Clan—the one Iroquois clan that did not participate in the killing of the Jesuits—he would have seen their heads upon the palisade wall and perhaps regretted what had happened. Eventually, he was chosen to be one of the chiefs of this village who made important decisions for the Iroquois at the main council fire at Onondaga. He must have had the leadership qualities that the Iroquois deemed important, as described in their Great Law of Peace:

> The chiefs of the League of Five Nations shall be mentors of the people for all time. The thickness of their skin shall be seven spans, which is to say that they shall be proof against anger, offensive action, and criticism. Their hearts shall be full of peace and good will and their minds filled with a yearning for the welfare of the people of the League. With endless patience, they shall carry out their duty. Their firmness shall be tempered with a tenderness for their people. Neither anger nor fury shall find lodging in their minds, and all their words and actions shall be marked by calm deliberation.[8]

Though we don't know the name of Tekakwitha's father, as a Mohawk chief he would have been an important leader of their time, for the Mohawk tribe was instrumental in all decision making for the Iroquois League. Article 6 of the Great Law of Peace of the Iroquois states that no council was legal unless all the Mohawk chiefs were present, and nothing could be passed if the Mohawks disagreed. Since Tekakwitha's father was of the Turtle Clan, he was a key deliberator at the council in the role of Firekeeper, a major decision-making role. Only three Mohawk chiefs held this position at one time.

In the biographical accounts written by the Jesuit missionaries about Tekakwitha's life, there is no mention of the names of Tekakwitha's parents; however, we do know that her mother was from the Algonquin tribe and was baptized at Three Rivers. Exactly how Tekakwitha's grandparents came to faith is unknown, but the Algonquin were heavily evangelized by the Jesuits and many converts had been made among them. Through the efforts of the Jesuits, Tekakwitha's grandparents must have converted and had their daughter baptized sometime between 1634 and 1639.

Perhaps Tekakwitha's grandparents' conversion followed a similar path as this story recorded by Jesuit missionary Fr. Paul Le Jeune, who built the chapel in which Tekakwitha's mother was baptized:

> A woman told us not long ago that, being sick, the thought occurred to her that there must be someone who could cure her; she invokes him, she recovers her health. "Some time after that," said she, "I went down to Quebec; I heard you speak of God and of his Omnipotence; I immediately began to say in my heart, 'This is he to whom I have prayed, and who has cured me. I did not know his name, I did not understand him; I must listen to what is said of him, in order to believe in him.'"[9]

This disposition among some of the Native Americans is part of what spread the message of Christ, especially to the Algonquin and Huron, whose native territory was on the northern side of the St. Lawrence River where the Jesuits built the missions. They desired baptism and rejected several violent and cruel native customs. A young Algonquin warrior also approached Fr. Le Juene, seeking God. The warrior had been spared from death despite having contracted a serious disease.

He remarked, "There must certainly be in the Universe some powerful spirit which has preserved me; for I have done nothing for my recovery more than the others, and yet my body is not made of a different material. I would gladly know this benefactor." This young warrior came upon the Jesuits at their mission in Quebec and listened intently as they taught about God in the Algonquin language. His heart burned with desire to learn more as he listened to the twice-daily lessons of the Jesuits and spent time in the chapel in meditation. With enthusiasm, he shared what he learned with his kinsmen.[10] He said to Fr. Le Juene that there must be a great workman behind even the simple concept of a hand's ability to open and close.

The preknowledge of God that this warrior exhibited is explained in the *Catechism of the Catholic Church*, 35:

> Man's faculties make him capable of coming to a knowledge of the existence of a personal God. But for man to be able to enter into real intimacy with him, God willed both to reveal himself to man and to give him the grace of being able to welcome this revelation in faith. The proofs of God's existence, however, can predispose one to faith and help one to see that faith is not opposed to reason.

This short paragraph of the *Catechism* is played out in real time during this period of conversion of the Huron and Algonquin tribes. Many found that what the Jesuits were teaching was something that their hearts called out for. The Jesuits were able to connect these seekers to the God in whom they already believed, yet did not understand. The revelation of Jesus Christ brought them answers and a new way of life. While still keeping many of their native customs of food and dress, many Native Americans settled near Jesuit missions in order to live in a Christian community. Tekakwitha's Algonquin mother grew up at one such settlement at Three Rivers. She, like this young warrior, would have listened to the lessons of the Jesuits, attended Mass, learned the rosary, and spent hours in prayer and meditation.

How Tekakwitha's mother became a Mohawk was an ordeal many others of her tribe also underwent. As a young lady, she was aware of the threat of Mohawk raids into her homeland, such as the raid that captured Fr. Jogues. By this time, the Mohawks had almost completely annihilated her Algonquin people, and the fear of them was as tangible as the rushing St. Lawrence River from which the Mohawk warriors executed their attacks.

On an ominous day in the early 1650s, a large band of Mohawk warriors raided Three Rivers, carrying off a number of captives, including Tekakwitha's mother, who was in her late teens.[11] In the years following, the Iroquois League would completely destroy or assimilate both the Algonquin and Huron tribes in this way. As a result, many Christians were absorbed into the Iroquois League, although for the most part, their Catholic religious practices had to be abandoned.

The plight of Tekakwitha's mother as a Christian Algonquin captured by their enemy the Mohawks would certainly have been a terrifying experience. No doubt she and her fellow captives would have faced the traditional treatment of new initiates to the tribe, which could entail cutting off or breaking fingers, burning the soles of the feet, and beatings with clubs. One account of a similar raid recorded in *The Jesuit Relations* tells of a young woman so distraught about her capture and fearful of what she would have to endure that she hurled herself into an icy river rather than face certain torture.[12] The tribes of the Northern Woodlands had similar practices, though the Mohawks were the most feared because of their bold forays across the Northeast.

The Mohawks brought captives into their tribes when their population numbers were down and the work force needed to be bolstered. The women clan leaders would decide when this type of war was necessary, and then raiding warriors would leave the village to capture their enemies. Captives were brought back to serve as slaves, and those who endured the tortures could be accepted into the tribe as full members—considered to be Mohawks, no matter their tribe of birth. These types of wars were called "mourning wars" because the tribe could assuage its grief over their lost loved ones by replacing the missing with new members who were strong yet compliant.

Tekakwitha's mother endured the three-hundred-mile journey by water and land into what must have seemed a deep wilderness after being raised in a French settlement. She must have considered her fate along the way and spent the time reciting the prayers she had known by heart since a child.

By the time she arrived at the outskirts of the town of Ossernenon,[13] her husband-to-be was already a chief of the village. With his status, he probably was able to choose her as his wife right away, rather than subjecting her to tortures and slavery like many of the others. Those who were sturdy, cooperative, and brave were typically adopted into the tribe, whereas those who showed cowardice were usually killed on the spot. Some remained in the tribe as slaves to do the menial tasks of fetching firewood or water.

It would have been evident to her new husband that Tekakwitha's mother was a Christian, since he knew from where the new captives had come. It was becoming commonplace for an Iroquois tribe to have a good percentage of Christian Huron and Algonquin among them due to similar raids. Finding a fellow Christian would have been comforting for the young woman, however the open practice of the Catholic faith would not have been part of their lives other than prayer. It is most likely that she and other Christians did not participate in parts of the Mohawk festivals that the Jesuits considered pagan.

Perhaps as Tekakwitha's mother listened to the oral tales of her new tribe, she would have heard the story of how St. Isaac Jogues had lived among them for a while and eventually had been killed at their hands. She now lived among people who were opposed to all she had ever known as a Christian Algonquin and as an ally of the French, the Iroquois's bitter enemy. Now as a full member of the Mohawk tribe, she had to live within the new parameters.

Certainly one comfort that she clung to from her life among the Christians would have been praying the rosary, since it could be done without disrupting the pattern of life. Beads were a big part of Native American women's lives, worn as ornaments and decorations on clothing and they were very adept at sewing beadwork to clothing and moccasins. They also made strings of beads from glass obtained through trade with the Dutch, or from shells or wampum, so, if Tekakwitha's mother had made her own glass bead rosary, it would not have been out of place. The rosaries distributed by the Jesuits had medals or crosses attached to them, and several of these medals have been found during excavations throughout the Mohawk Valley where Jesuits were present. These findings were used to help date the archaeological sites.[14]

Tekakwitha's mother and the other Christian captives were like dormant seeds waiting for the water of the Holy Spirit to nurture them. They waited with hope that the Jesuits would make their way into Iroquois territory to set up missions among them, as they had done among so many other Native American tribes. Waiting and praying, waiting and praying, all the while holding firm to their belief in Jesus Christ. Yet, surrounding them, the native Mohawks continued their raids and attacks on the French and their Native American allies, making their name a fearful and odious one.

Chapter Two

EARLY LIFE: TEKAKWITHA THE SURVIVOR
1656–1666

In 1656, Tekakwitha was born in the longhouse of her father's Turtle Clan in the village of Ossernenon.[1] Like all babies of the time, she would have been strapped to a wooden cradle board carved with floral decorations and carried by her mother out into the fields surrounding their village during the planting and harvesting of the Native American staples of corn, beans, and squash.

Perhaps her cradleboard was suspended from a nearby tree as her mother labored in the field, and Tekakwitha could observe the beauty of the world from her secure cocoon. She would have been loved and prized by her extended family as they watched her grow. They may have watched with amused approval as she carried a branch toward the cooking fire like she saw other children do, all the while learning the importance of being part of a tribe. She would feel the security of the longhouse, where she was bundled in furs during the long winter nights, listening to the crackling fire and watching the animated story-tellers as they filled the longhouse with waving shadows, amazing expressions, chants, and songs.

Soon a baby brother was born to the family, and Tekakwitha's mother would have proved herself valuable to the tribe, with two healthy children and her contribution of hard work.

Around the time of Tekakwitha's birth, there was a short period between 1655 and 1658 in which the Iroquois allowed the Jesuit missionaries to visit their villages, just as the Christians had hoped and prayed. Tekakwitha's mother would have rejoiced to see them again, to hear news about those she had known at Three Rivers, to absorb stories about Jesus and Mary, and to pray.

At a central location in Onondaga territory, several miles west of Mohawk territory, a mission was built called St. Marie Among the Iroquois, from which Jesuit priests traveled to serve the surrounding tribes. Fr. Simon Le Moyne visited the villages in the Mohawk Valley, with the mutual understanding that he was visiting those who were already Christians.

The Jesuit Relations records an incident of a Huron Christian woman, a captive of six years, waiting outside of a village for the priest to arrive so he could baptize her small child. Her words expressed the collective feeling of the Christians living among the Iroquois when she said, "Your coming makes us glad in our inmost souls; our smallest children are so rejoiced that they begin to grow before our eyes; and even those not yet born leap with joy in their mothers' wombs, and wish to come forth at the earliest moment to be blessed in seeing you."[2]

The eagerness that this woman felt regarding her child's baptism would also have been the sentiment of Tekakwitha's mother, but for her to ask a visiting Jesuit for baptism for her children would not have been acceptable, due to her status as the wife of a chief. She would have been allowed to participate, however, in a Mass said outside of the village with the other Christians. The visit from Fr. Le Moyne most likely gave a glimmer of life to Tekakwitha's mother—a hope that the Jesuits setting up a permanent mission in Iroquois territory meant that someday permission for her children to be baptized would be granted by her tribe. What she could offer her children now were her constant prayers. She was known in the village as a woman of prayer, and the image of her kneeling each evening to pray may have been one that Tekakwitha had etched in her memory.

The mission among the Iroquois did not last long, however, as it came to light that the Onondaga's purpose for allowing the Jesuits to set up the mission was actually a plot to kill them all. In 1658, when word of this slipped out through a dying man, the missionaries were summoned back to headquarters in Quebec. Fifty-three of them fled for their lives back to Canada while the Onondaga were sleeping. There would be a gap of ten years before the Jesuits returned to the Iroquois, so Tekakwitha grew up in an environment firm in its traditional Mohawk practices, with only subtle whispers of Christianity among the captive population.

DEADLY EPIDEMIC

In 1659 Tekakwitha's village planned to rebuild in another location—a common practice for the Iroquois when the ground was no longer fertile for farming.[3] They would clear a section of forest, usually on a bluff overlooking the Mohawk River, using the trees and bark to build their longhouses and to construct the palisade walls around the village. The Europeans called these villages "castles."

Tekakwitha's father and a few other Mohawk chiefs approached their Dutch neighbors living at Fort Orange to request their assistance. They asked for horses to help pull the logs to the building site, for a cannon, and for renewed friendship. Several beaver skins were given to the Dutch during the proceedings, and in response, a Dutch delegation came to the Mohawk villages carrying gifts of wampum, gunpowder, lead, axes, and knives. It was not often that the Dutch ventured into Iroquois territory, as they preferred the Native Americans to come to their trading post on the Hudson River.

The arrival of the Dutch delegation, however, coincided with a severe outbreak of smallpox among the villages where the Dutch had visited. Smallpox may also have reached the villages through trade items like wool for blankets and clothing. Before the new village was constructed, when Tekakwitha was four years old, her village succumbed to this deadly disease, and one by one, each longhouse was filled with suffering people. They would first contract a rash, followed a few days later by raised pustules over all of the body, often most densely upon the face. Fluid then would drain from the lesions, and after a week or so, scabs would form, which, when they fell off, left the signature pockmarks behind.

Since the victims were too ill to fetch water or food, they could only lie down, and their lesions would adhere to the mats and pull off their skin if they tried to roll over. With so many sick, there were few to care for them, and at Ossernenon, upwards of 60 percent of the inhabitants died.[4] This scenario played out over and over again throughout the Native American communities, wiping out an estimated 80 percent of their population in the mid-seventeenth century.[5] Among the dead were Tekakwitha's parents.

The scourge of smallpox affected Tekakwitha in a profound way. It left her an orphan at age four, and it scarred her body and face with pockmarks and nearly ruined her eyesight. She may have also suffered ill health throughout her lifetime due to the after effects of the disease, contributing to her death at a young age. As she recovered from the disease, she took refuge in the longhouse, where the light did not hurt her eyes and the scars on her face were not as noticeable.[6]

Tekakwitha's baby brother also perished during the epidemic. The mortality rate for infants and elderly was the highest, leaving the Native American populations without their elders, who held the oral traditions and knowledge of their customs and crafts. In a matter of weeks, unrecoverable information was lost. Despite this devastation, those who recovered continued to build their new village, and a small remnant reassembled at their new town they called Caughnawaga, which means "by the rapids." The Native Americans had learned that it was not safe to live in the same surroundings where people had died from the mysterious disease, so after moving to their new town, they burned their old village to the ground.

As was the custom of the Iroquois, immediate family took on the care of orphans. Tekakwitha was taken into the care of her father's brother, who was also a chief in their village. Perhaps he had escaped the smallpox epidemic because he was away on a hunting party for the duration of the contagious period. He and his wife had no children of their own, or perhaps they had lost them in the epidemic. Tekakwitha's aunt and uncle also adopted another girl who was older than Tekakwitha. Their new parents and another aunt continued to raise them in all the ways of the Mohawk tribe.

We do not know how much Tekakwitha recalled of her Christian mother, or how much she may have learned of Catholic practice, but we can surmise that she heard from other Christians in her tribe what they knew of her mother and her faith. Fr. Chauchetiere recounts in his biography of Tekakwitha that her mother had prayed until her death.[7] A topic surely to have been discussed among Tekakwitha's tribe was the Mohawks' mistrust of the Jesuits. She heard stern warnings about the danger of following them and stories about how evil curses, sickness, and death were linked to the sign of the cross and baptism.

It does appear, however, that the Mohawks allowed Christians to pray and to be excluded from some practices that the Jesuits had prohibited converts to perform, including torture and mutilation of captives, cannibalism, promiscuity, and participating in dream festivals, which the Jesuits believed was linked to sorcery.[8] It was customary for even the youngest Mohawk children to join in such practices, but as Tekakwitha's mother had not participated in them, Tekakwitha would not have been exposed to them as a young child. In the account of St. Isaac Jogues, when he was strapped as a captive to an elm plank, young children threw embers from the fire onto his chest. Tekakwitha did not show cruelty to anyone and was grieved deeply when others were harmed.[9] Her desire to avoid these practices could be one reason why she took solace in the longhouse.

Another reason was her need to avoid bright light. Her sensitive eyes made it necessary to cover her head with a blanket when she was outdoors in order not to be blinded by sunlight. Even with her damaged eyesight, Tekakwitha learned the crafts of the Iroquois, such as weaving wampum belts and embroidering clothing with moose hair and quills. Her biographers commented on her skills and industrious spirit as she grew older. Fr. Chauchetiere wrote:

> The people who knew her as a small child said that she had spirit and was skillful, especially with her fingers, in making such objects as the other Natives do. If I would judge from the objects that I saw her make, I say with ease that she had worked skillfully in porcupine and moose skins. She made belts that the Native women would carry and wood and wampum belts made of shell beads, which the elders used in negotiating the affairs of the nation. Another occupation of the Native women was the sewing that they had learned from both the slaves who were with them or the women from Europe. She was skillful in making ribbons, which the Natives make from eel skins or tree barks. These she colored red with the glue from sturgeons, which is often employed among the Iroquois. She knew more than the

Iroquois girls because she made baskets and buckets used to carry water. In this manner, her skills had always kept her with something to be occupied with. She sometimes made a hollow tree trunk for grinding corn, mats from tree bark, and poles to stack the corn. Her everyday occupations were to peel the corn, to make the sagamite and the Native bread, search for water, carry wood and also fill the plates with food and serve them.[10]

As we can see from this description, Tekakwitha was well trained in the natural arts of food preparation and handicrafts. She wore the traditional clothing of her people, which by this time in history included wool and cloth from the Europeans instead of the buckskin of her predecessors. It was much easier to obtain cloth for clothes through trading than it was to prepare deer hide, so European fabric was used to make Iroquois traditional-style clothing.

A typical outfit for Iroquois women was described by a Dutchman living nearby at the time of Tekakwitha's birth: loose-fitting cloth blouses embroidered on the chest with beads, a buckskin skirt with petticoat beneath, leather leggings, and ornately beaded moccasins. One source mentions that the blanket Tekakwitha wore about her shoulders was crimson.[11] Fr. Chauchetiere mentioned that she wore a shell necklace around her neck and bracelets on her arms, rings, and earrings. Around her waist was a shell bead belt, and in her hair were ribbons of colored eel skin.[12]

The common way for women to wear their hair was to part it in the middle and bring it all to the back in a braid. For married women, the hair was left unbraided but gathered at the back and folded like a beaver tail and secured with ribbon or covered with an embroidered scarf.[13] Tekakwitha may have been more finely adorned than some girls of her age because she was the daughter of a chief. Young girls often arrayed themselves in beads and embroidery to attract boys—a practice encouraged by the adults of the village. It was customary to pledge children to marry at a very young age—at age eight for Tekakwitha— however neither she nor the boy involved were the least bit interested.

JESUIT PROHIBITIONS

The Iroquois had many seasonal festivals throughout the year that would last for several days. Tekakwitha would have been involved in these to some extent; however, her timid demeanor kept her from joining in—especially parts of the mid-winter festival in which dream guessing and interpretation was a large part. People would often reenact their dreams and encourage others to play roles in the reenactment. Dreams were a sort of reality in the Native American way of thinking, and it was critical that a person understand or fulfill their dreams for their health and well-being.[14]

The Jesuits forbade this. They considered it sorcery because it was not the spirit of God leading them to act out the odd scenarios of their dreams. The *Catechism of the Catholic Church* explains that position in paragraph 2117:

> All practices of *magic* or *sorcery*, by which one attempts to tame occult powers, so as to place them at one's service and have a supernatural power over others—even if this were for the sake of restoring their health—are gravely contrary to the virtue of religion. These practices are even more to be condemned when accompanied by the intention of harming someone, or when they have recourse to the intervention of demons. Wearing charms is also reprehensible. *Spiritism* often implies divination or magical practices; the Church for her part warns the faithful against it. Recourse to so-called traditional cures does not justify either the invocation of evil powers or the exploitation of another's credulity.

For the same reason, the Jesuits were opposed to the False Face Society, which they thought used occult powers to conjure healing rather than the power of God. Members of this group wore large wooden masks carved from a tree whose spirit, they believed, had spoken to them. The masks had large eyes, crooked noses, and intimidating expressions to scare away bad spirits. They were highly polished and decorated with feathers or long hair made of cornhusks. These masks were considered sacred because they contained the power of a spirit they called "The Grandfather." The story of how the Grandfather received his power was retold during these ceremonies.

During a healing ceremony, the mask wearers vigorously shook turtle rattles and blew wood ashes over the afflicted. The ceremony also included the burning of tobacco and the eating of sagamite, and as tokens of thanks, those healed gave gifts of tobacco and corn. The Native Americans believed that by frightening away the bad spirits, good spirits could then enter the house of the sick person. The seven-day mid-winter festival that marked the beginning of a new year began with the masked False Face members stirring the ashes in each hearth in the longhouses and included prayers of thanks, sacred dances, and the sacrifice of a white dog to symbolize the removal of evil from the community.

Dream guessing—again prohibited by the Jesuits—also played a major role in Iroquois society. Though the use of dreams in the Bible was common—such as the account of God's prompting St. Joseph in a dream to lead his family to safety in Egypt after the birth of Christ— the Native American practices of dream interpreting were unacceptable because they seemed to be induced by demons, and morality was often put aside to fulfill them.

One such recorded instance from *The Jesuit Relations*, Vol. 42, illustrates how unsettling dream interpretation could become. Two priests on a missionary journey in 1655 traveled with a group of Native Americans. One evening, one of the Native Americans awoke at midnight, crying out and panting, tossing like a madman. Many ran to him to see if he was ill, but he cried in a frenzy all the more, frightening them so that they hid their weapons from him. He then jumped up and leaped into the river, thrashing about until some pulled him back out. Finally he told them he had dreamed that a water animal had jumped into his stomach and to rid himself of the creature he had plunged into the river. As was customary, to bring his mind back to soundness, his dream had to be relived by the others. So with many voices imitating ducks and frogs, they sat in a sweat lodge until he felt better and was able to fall back to sleep. The concluding comment by the writer was, "He who deals with pagan Savages is in danger of losing his life through a dream."[15]

The Jesuits also wanted to keep the new converts from other sins, such as the evil practices mentioned in Galatians 5:20: "Now the works of the flesh are plain: fornication, impurity, licentiousness, idolatry, sorcery, enmity, strife, jealousy, anger, selfishness, dissension, factions, envy, drunkenness, carousing, and the like. I warn you, as I warned you before, that those who do such things shall not inherit the kingdom of God."

This strong admonishment was impressed upon new converts. The Jesuits worked hard to disentangle the convert from many native practices, many times unsuccessfully. One reason St. Kateri stands out among other converts was her ability to resist these practices that the Jesuits taught were against the faith.

INVASION

When Tekakwitha was about ten years old, her tribe endured a trial nearly as great as the smallpox epidemic. Throughout her lifetime, the

Iroquois and the French had been at odds. The French had made allies of the Huron, who were enemies of the Iroquois, and because of their alliance, the Iroquois had no qualms about attacking French settlements and taking captives. This was not acceptable to the governors of New France, so negotiations and peace talks began between New France and the Iroquois. Unfortunately, due to miscommunications and lack of cooperation by the Mohawks, the French determined the only way to stop the raiding was by invading Mohawk territory.

In the fall of 1666, Tekakwitha sat within the shelter of her family longhouse as the rain pelted down upon the high, arching roof during a prolonged storm. Women were preparing meals of cooked corn or wild game, while children played with sticks and stones nearby. Tekakwitha was beyond the age of idle playtime and was busily practicing the skill of embroidery learned from her aunts, when suddenly the entire house stopped their chores at the shout of alarm by a group of young warriors. Their animated message filled the villagers with dread: "The army of the French is on its way here! We saw them with Algonquin marching toward our valley to attack! They are marching even through the night to reach us!"

Immediately the whole village was on alert, and an evacuation plan went into effect. The women and children would flee, while the men would stay to defend the village. Tekakwitha and the women of her clan hastily grabbed what they could carry, and as the evacuation plan was set in motion, Tekakwitha was caught in its current. She hoisted her bundle of belongings onto her back and adjusted the burden strap across her forehead,[16] which helped to bear the weight of her load. Perhaps she carried her embroidery tools and supplies of beads, shells, and porcupine quills, or perhaps mats she had woven or wool blankets or dried corn.

After one last look down the now dark longhouse, she would have hurried toward the exit of Caughnawaga through the wooden palisade walls,[17] following behind her clan members as they hastily filtered into the nearby woodland. Her village of 370 Mohawks now disbursed rapidly into the drenched forest on foot, or perhaps some escaped by canoe along the nearby Mohawk River, paddling swiftly to safety and hiding the canoes from view. A string of women and children raced through the forest along a familiar path that led west toward the largest Mohawk village to the west.[18] There they could take shelter in the main castle, while the warriors defended Caughnawaga using traditional weapons of bow and arrow and tomahawk, as well as several muskets they had obtained through trade with the Dutch.

The French army was approaching over land from Lake George to the north with six hundred French soldiers, six hundred settlers, and a band of one hundred Huron and Algonquins.[19] This was their second attempt to attack the Mohawks within the year. Their first attempt in the frigid winter had left many soldiers dead from cold, hunger, and Mohawk attack. The French, under the command of Lieutenant-General Marquis de Tracy, were attacking again because of the constant raiding of the Mohawks into New France and their refusal to make peace like some of the other Iroquois nations had done.

But in this second attempt, the French army was twice the size and more determined than ever to defeat the Mohawks. The warriors who stayed behind to defend Caughnawaga had little time to plan how to protect their homes and harvest. When they heard the drumming of the steadily approaching French army, they panicked and fled after the others, fearing they were far outnumbered. Before long, the sinister glow against the gray sky told the Mohawks that their village was ablaze, destroying their homes, harvest storage, and anything left behind. The village of Caughnawaga was one of several Iroquois villages dotted along the Mohawk River. It was clear now to the remaining villages that they too were in danger from the avenging French army.

Once again Tekakwitha swiftly escaped into the forest, perhaps this time heading for a temporary campsite used in the winter by hunting parties when the snow lay several feet deep and game could be easily tracked. The threat of facing the winter without adequate food reserves and insufficient shelter was the reality for these displaced people. This moment of uncertainty was but a symbol of the uncertainty of the future of the Iroquois. For millennia these people had lived in much the same way, migrating here or there and clashing with one tribe or another, but never had there been foreign armies with large numbers invading their territory. Though the Mohawks were resilient and resourceful, the push of the Europeans was changing their world. All of the villages in the Mohawk Valley were plundered and burned to the ground. De Tracy commented in his journal that there was enough food stored in the villages to feed all of Canada for two years.[20] All they left behind was a wooden cross in the ground to show the land belonged to France.

Tekakwitha may have looked at this cross and wondered about its meaning. Christians had crosses. The French were Christian. The French burned her town to the ground.

Over the winter, many of the Mohawks died of starvation and exposure. Tekakwitha and her family survived, and they were part of the remnant that built a new village of Caughnawaga,[21] not far from the one destroyed by the French just to the north across the Mohawk River. Every tribe member had a task to perform, such as harvesting bark for the protective covering attached to the bent saplings that formed the rounded roof over the beam framework of the longhouse—yet it would be a long struggle to recover from so great a blow.

In the springtime, the women labored in the newly cleared land surrounding the village to plant the traditional Native American crops. They gathered the soil into mounds and planted the three types of seeds all together in one mound where the plants grew together like three sisters: tall corn supported the creeping bean plants, while the squash covered the ground beneath. With great hopes for a bountiful harvest, the villagers carried on their traditional festivals. Faithfully the earth yielded the sweet berries in the spring, as though to say she would take care of them for yet another year.

With gratitude, the women canvassed the sunny spots where strawberries grew and gathered them into their baskets. The occasion of the spring berries was met with a festival in thanksgiving in which sweet drinks of strawberry juice mixed with maple sugar were shared. No doubt this harvest meant a lot to the recovering tribe, who was slowly gaining strength after the winter with meager rations. This group of survivors carried on the traditions of their people with a celebration of games and dancing.

A CONFLICT OF CULTURES

Tekakwitha's uncle, a leader of his village, was faced with a great task to try to help his family and tribe from disappearing from their lands as had the Huron and Algonquin and many other tribes of whom there is no historical record. In order to do so, he would have to do as his ancestors before him had done, by upholding the ways and customs that had made the Mohawks so strong originally.

Subjugating enemies through warfare and the staunch adherence to tradition was his job as chief, however the living situation in his village was not conducive to those methods, even in his own family. His adopted daughters had already been raised partly in the Christian tradition, so to be too harsh with Christian practice was difficult. His task became even harder over time, as the influx of Christian captives increased.

And yet he was a traditional Mohawk, proud of their ways. He dressed with long leather breeches, a loincloth, and moccasins. He proudly wore the headdress of three eagle feathers that identified him as a Mohawk. It was made of strips of ash wood: one that encircled the head and one strip that attached to the band from front to back on which small holes would be drilled in order to secure feathers to it. For certain occasions, Tekakwitha's uncle and other men painted their faces and shaved their heads, leaving a portion of their hair long.

He also would have carried a tobacco pipe with him to be used during times of discussion or decision making. Pipes were made of stone, bone, or clay, and tobacco was grown for ceremonial purposes, usually within the village. Not only was it smoked in pipes, it was thrown into the fire as a ceremonial offering on many important occasions. The aroma of the tobacco was a cue to Tekakwitha that her uncle was deep in thought. And those times would have been many.

Tekakwitha's uncle carried a great weight. He was a diplomat among his own people, trying to keep the tribe cohesive by allowing the Christians to pray while at the same time encouraging the festivals and customs that made the Mohawks who they were. He was also a diplomat to the Europeans, as he tried to appease the French who now had the upper hand. He made trading transactions with first the Dutch and later the British, while maintaining Iroquois dominance of the fur trade by keeping at bay the enemy tribes east of the Hudson River.

Tekakwitha was always respectful of her uncle and feared him enough not to cross his wishes for her to remain a traditional Mohawk, but within her heart was always the pull toward the beliefs and ways of her Christian mother.

Chapter Three

TEKAKWITHA MEETS THE BLACK ROBES

1667–1675

After the devastation of the Mohawk villages by the French army, an envoy of Mohawks and Oneidas met in Quebec with the French to bring gifts of peace and to escort Jesuit missionaries back to their nations as part of the peace terms. This was met with mixed emotions among the people at the new Caughnawaga. The Christians looked with joy for the coming of the "Black Robes," as they were called, while the others probably felt resentment, seeing the new customs of the Jesuits as dangerous and detrimental to the survival of traditional Mohawk life.

Though the coming of the Black Robes brought suspicion and resistance, some amount of tolerance was necessary due to the Mohawk's vulnerable position with the French. And as time passed, the attitude toward Christianity moved from mistrust to tolerance to acceptance, although the number of Mohawk converts was still a minority.

Jesuit authority had vastly changed over the years. When St. Isaac Jogues came to Ossernenon the first time, the Iroquois were the mightiest nation in the northeast. Now they were depopulated by disease and war, diffused through the assimilation of other Native American tribes who were mostly Christian, and greatly weakened from the devastation of their villages by the French. In 1642, an Iroquois could behead a Frenchman with no repercussions, but in 1667 the might of the French army made it clear that things had changed. The threat of death for a Black Robe was now unlikely. They were seen not only as Christian missionaries, but also as an extension of the great power of France.

NEW FRIENDSHIP

On a hot July afternoon in 1667, when Tekakwitha was about eleven years old, she had her first experience with Jesuit missionaries. It was fitting that they first went to the group of Mohawks who had martyred St. Isaac Jogues and his companions, and this would open a new chapter in Mohawk-Jesuit relations.

Three priests—Fr. Jacques Bruyas, Fr. Jacques Fremin, and Fr. Jean Pierron—had been chosen to preach the faith to the Iroquois and to encourage them to abandon their violent attacks on European settlers. The envoy had been scheduled to arrive at the main Mohawk castle of Tionondogen, but apparently everyone there was drunk and in no shape to receive them. In the spirit of hospitality, Tekakwitha's uncle brought them into his longhouse, where Tekakwitha was sitting. She brought the missionaries the traditional cooked corn dish of sagamite, and attended to them during their stay.

The many villagers in Caughnawaga who were already Christians were thrilled to have priests among them to administer the sacraments. For some, it may have been more than a decade since they had seen a Black Robe, and the privilege to attend Mass and gather for morning and evening prayer would have buoyed their spirits. The missionaries also made the rounds of the longhouses, looking for any sick they could assist.

On Fr. Fremin's first visit to the Mohawk village, he came across a woman who had recently been attacked and scalped by an enemy Mohegan. She lay on a mat in a longhouse, bleeding from her grievous wound. After the defeat of the Mohawks by the French, the neighboring tribes, with the leadership of the Mohegans, thought they could gain the upper hand over their rivals and made many assaults on Mohawk villages. It was dangerous for Mohawk women to work in the fields outside the palisade walls, and the women of Caughnawaga had to be the most vigilant because their town was the furthest east and the first to be reached by enemies penetrating Mohawk territory.

Fr. Fremin told her of the promise of heaven if she agreed to be baptized. She was resistant to him, but after four tries and the fervent prayers of the other Frenchmen in the envoy, she repeated the prayers and was baptized before she died.

Another Mohawk woman requested that she and her infant son be baptized, and Fr. Fremin selected her to be in charge of the Christian group to notify them of meeting and prayer times. Tekakwitha was able to observe the group of Christians at their prayers and felt very positive toward the Black Robes and their practices.[1]

After three days, the French envoy left for the main castle of Tionondogen in a solemn procession of two hundred Mohawk men. The villagers welcomed them with artillery fire into the air and a speech by a great orator, who expressed the hope that the French would continue in peaceful friendship and that they would help them fight against the Mohegans.

A few months later, the men, women, and children of all the neighboring Mohawk villages assembled at Tionondogen to hear the terms offered the Mohawk by the French. Fr. Fremin had erected a very tall pole with a necklace of wampum hanging at the top. He admonished them for their raids on French settlements and the mistreatment of certain government officials. He assured them of the friendship offered by the French and explained their goal to help the tribes live like Christians. In this way, they could be accepted as subjects of the King of France and be under his protection. After a moment of silence, he continued, directing their attention to the tall pole: "The first Iroquois to kill a Frenchman or his allies will be hanged like this!"

The Mohawks stood in astonishment, with their heads bowed. Finally, the Mohawk orator rose up and walked around the pole with animated gestures until finally he grabbed his throat and illustrated dramatically the severity of this message. He then gave an eloquent speech, accepting the terms of the French—which included the release of several Mohawk-held captives—and offered to build the Jesuits a chapel. As everyone returned home after this pivotal meeting, it was evident that the Jesuits would now be influential in Mohawk decision making.

While the other priests moved on to minister elsewhere, Fr. Fremin stayed on at Tionondogen to set up a permanent mission. He built a chapel called St. Marie with the enthusiastic help of the Natives.

Around the same time, a mission in New France was established by Fr. Pierre Rafeix adjacent to the French settlement of La Prairie, near Montreal. This mission would become significant in the life of Tekakwitha because, as Christians learned of the mission at La Prairie, which later relocated to Sault St. Louis, many would leave Iroquois country to go and join with the growing Christian community where they could live a Christian life without persecution.[2] It was only a matter of time before Mohawk converts from Caughnawaga would also move there.

TRIBES AT WAR, BLACK ROBES IN ACTION

Yet the path was never without complication. Shortly after Fr. Fremin had baptized the woman he had selected to oversee prayers at Tionondogen, a string of unfortunate events befell her, including the illness of her son and the death of her husband at the hand of the

Mohegans. The villagers blamed the woman's baptism for these trag-edies. They reviled her and mistreated her for eight days, but she held firm to her faith.

Next, her eyes swelled shut and the villagers again harassed her to give up her faith and submit to the False Face medicine society with their chants and shaking turtle rattles, but she refused. Finally, they left her alone. She and her son recovered their health, and she continued to faithfully teach her son to pray.[3] This ever-present tug back and forth between the firm faith of the Christians and the staunch belief in the traditional ways of the Iroquois was often repeated. Well aware of where her uncle stood on the issue, Tekakwitha as yet expressed no desire to follow the Black Robes.

In the spring of 1668, a delegation of Mohawks departed for Quebec, bearing gifts for the Governor of New France to request help against the Mohegans and to ask for more Black Robes. As a result, Fr. Pierron was sent to relieve the overworked Fr. Fremin, who went to work with the Seneca. Fr. Pierron made a circuit of the Mohawk villages, visiting them every eight days. This meant that Tekakwitha would have observed Fr. Pierron in Caughnawaga during his travels when he would bring his paintings that showed in a powerful way the options of life after death. The image of the fires of hell was one the tribe could relate to well, since they used fire as a way to punish their enemies, and their respect for the Black Robes grew.

A group of men built a longhouse-style chapel for Fr. Pierron and the Christians, which they named St. Peter. Fr. Pierron also began to instruct the Mohawks using card games and symbols that taught the seven sacraments, the virtues, and the ten commandments.

But the threat of the Mohegans always loomed large for the tribes, and their apprehension over this threat became a reality one morning in the summer of 1669. The village of Caughnawaga was attacked by the Mohegans, starting with a barrage of bullets coming through the walls into the longhouses themselves. The warriors of the town rallied quickly at the platforms of the palisades to defend the town, and the women and children stood ready with weapons in case the walls should be breached. For several days, the Mohegans surrounded the town with six hundred warriors, but ran out of ammunition and eventually retreated.

The Mohawks were determined to drive the Mohegans out of Mohawk territory and were led by a war-chief known as "The Great Mohawk." They met on the battlefield of Kinaquariones, and the Mohawks were able to maintain the upper hand, killing the Mohegan war-chief Chickatawbut and other strategic leaders of their enemy. This victory, of course, led to torturing the captives that they brought back to Caughnawaga in large number. Fr. Pierron could not stop the Mohawks from torturing the Mohegans and eating their flesh. He was allowed, however, to spend a few days with the suffering captives and explain the faith to them. Each of them received baptism before they were killed. Surely Tekakwitha would have despaired the plight of the captives, but perhaps she took a bit of comfort that they at least could hear the Gospel first.

Another incident reflecting the inroads of the Jesuits occurred during the Festival of the Dead, which was celebrated every ten years by the Iroquois. During this celebration, the bones of all those who had died over the past ten years were collected and reburied in a mass grave outside the main village. This ceremony may have included the bones of Tekakwitha's parents. She attended with all the Mohawks from the surrounding villages, as did Fr. Pierron, who had been invited by the elders because of his dedication to the Mohawks.[4] Leaders from the other Iroquois tribes had also come, as was the custom.

As the ceremony progressed, the traditional stories were recited by one of the Mohawk chiefs, but, in a total break of protocol, Fr. Pierron spoke out against the story because it was against Catholic teaching. An argument broke out between him and the chief, and Fr. Pierron was forced to leave the ceremony. Later, Fr. Pierron explained why he had objected to the stories, and the chief apologized and told him that there was a better way to present his concerns. So Fr. Pierron invited the elders to his dwelling and gave a long speech, completing it by throwing three armfuls of wampum before them. Each armful represented a request: first, to ask them to follow God and his laws; second, to reject medicine men from invoking demons; and third, to stop dances that he considered superstitious.

They listened, but this was a lot for them to consider. After two councils, they responded by saying it was a very difficult task to give up traditions they have had since their beginning, but they would try to receive his instructions on the faith in the chapel. Amazingly, the medicine men threw their turtle rattles into the fire and the villagers agreed to only perform dances that were approved by Fr. Pierron. With this declaration of allegiance to the religion of Jesus Christ, the atmosphere became favorable for conversion.

CHRISTIAN INFLUENCE GROWS IN THE VILLAGES

By now, Tekakwitha was a young lady completely eligible for marriage—the daughter of a chief, well-mannered, and industrious. Since husbands would move into the longhouses of their wives, the longhouse could also benefit from the added hunter, who could provide meat for the household. And so Tekakwitha's aunts took on their role as husband-finders and began to invite suitors to visit.

Averse to the whole idea, Tekakwitha intimated to her aunts that she did not want to marry. When they pressed the issue and invited a boy to her longhouse to sit with her, she abruptly ran out and hid among the corn. So absurd to the Iroquois was this notion to remain unwed that her family treated her harshly like a slave for a period of time, hoping she would relent. To them, Tekakwitha's refusal meant she did not care if the longhouse had enough meat, but in her heart she wanted no man for a husband. This disposition would grow even stronger as she grew to know that Christ could be her spouse. She remained gentle and did all she was asked until finally it was her aunts who relented and allowed her back into the longhouse.

When Fr. Francois Boniface replaced Fr. Pierron, the new priest continued teaching classes, using Fr. Pierron's paintings. In 1671, Fr. Boniface saw the fruit of his preaching and instruction, with the baptism of about sixty Mohawks. But, though the village had declared its allegiance to Christ a few years ago, there was still much opposition toward those who abandoned native practices. A woman named Anastasia, for example, had refused to marry a non-Christian man and had not allowed her ill daughter to be visited by the False Face society—actions that brought taunts and hostility. Yet, as the Christians learned more about the missions of the Jesuits in New France, free from the resistance of non-Christians, a group of more than fifty Christians decided to leave Caughnawaga, Anastasia among them. No doubt Tekakwitha witnessed the insults and accusations of betrayal shouted at the group. In the end, many chose not to leave their families, and only fifteen actually left—but they were the most devout teachers. With this open rupture, tension surely remained high in the village.

Several more converted, and Caughnawaga truly became a fruitful harvest from the seeds planted by the martyrs. The neighboring village of Tionondogen, however, was a difficult place for the Gospel to take root. The liberal flow of alcohol there continued to plague them—a problem much abated in Caughnawaga because of the strong Christian presence.

At Christmas, Fr. Boniface set up a crèche in the chapel, displaying baby Jesus on a bed of pine and surrounded by candles. The Natives clamored to be able to enter the chapel to see it on that cold morning, and perhaps Tekakwitha, overcome with curiosity, would have peered into the chapel to see the mysterious scene. The images of Christianity became commonplace even outside the chapel, as it became popular among the Christians to wear medals, crucifixes, and rosaries. Certainly members of Tekakwitha's longhouse adorned themselves with these sacramentals and openly prayed on their rosaries. A deep desire to know more about this faith was building in her heart—a longing that would lead her to a point where it consumed her every waking thought.

One day, the chief called the Great Mohawk had a disagreement with his Christian wife and left the village with another chief. When his daughter died soon after, his wife was insulted with claims that her baptism had caused the misfortune, yet she firmly continued with her prayers in the chapel and her participation in the sacraments.

One his journey, the Great Mohawk met a Christian couple who prayed their prayers aloud. He was impressed with the meaning of the words and memorized them. They traveled together to the Church of St. Francis Xavier at Sault St. Louis, where they met Fr. Fremin— their village priest from the past. When the chiefs asked to be baptized, he taught them for a period of time and then instructed them to go back to their homes and return with their families first before he would baptize them.

This again brought a stir to Caughnawaga, as their mighty war chief returned to get his wife and daughter. He greatly mourned his daughter's death, yet spoke to the whole village and the nearby village of Andagaron to convince a group of forty-two to go with him to the mission at Sault St. Louis. This exodus included the sister of Tekakwitha and her husband. It was difficult for the villagers and Christians alike.

Fr. Boniface accompanied the convoy as they set sail via canoe down the Mohawk River on their way to New France.[5] The non-Christians could not help but wonder what was to become of them all. Tekakwitha's uncle was distraught that the village would continue to hemorrhage, leaving them with no warriors for protection or hunters for provisions. In this dire situation, no doubt he kept a close eye on Tekakwitha, to ensure that she did not follow the way of the Christians.

Chapter Four

TEKAKWITHA'S CONVERSION
1677–1680

In 1674, Fr. Jacques de Lamberville was sent to Caughnawaga to help Fr. Bruyas, the only priest left after Fr. Boniface left for New France. Fr. De Lamberville was fully aware that he was going to serve the same group of villagers who, over thirty years, ago had killed three Jesuit missionaries. Many things had changed since then, however, and the seeds that had been sewn by the blood of the martyrs were now being harvested not only in that village, but in the surrounding ones, as well. An obstinate chief from the village of Tionondogen had converted, which was a huge breakthrough since he had strongly resisted the Christians.

Tekakwitha's contact with the Jesuit priests had remained minimal in the seven years they had spent among the Mohawk. She continued with her daily work, but probably took as many opportunities as she could to listen to Christian talk about "the prayer," as the Mohawks referred to Christianity.

Sometime after the arrival of Fr. De Lamberville, Tekakwitha went with a group of women into the forest to gather firewood, when she stumbled and injured her leg. Two women helped her back to her long-house and applied traditional medicine to her swollen leg. After a few days, however, her leg still prevented her from working outside, and she contented herself to remain in the longhouse doing small household chores that didn't entail moving about. Suddenly, in the doorway, she saw a black silhouette with a broad brimmed hat and a long robe standing motionless with the bright morning rays of sun flooding the longhouse behind him. Tekakwitha could not look for long before her eyes smarted in pain. The figure stepped into the longhouse, surprised to see anyone inside, as all the other tribe members were out harvesting in the fields.

It was Fr. De Lamberville, whom Tekakwitha had not yet met. One of Tekakwitha's companions told the priest that they were tending to Tekakwitha's injured leg.

"I felt drawn here by the spirit of God," Fr. De Lamberville told the women. "Is there something I can do for you?" he asked, hoping to be of some use, perhaps with a prayer.

Though Tekakwitha was timid, she somehow found the words to express aloud what she had been saying in her heart. She told him of her desire to become a Christian, but qualified it with her worries about her uncle's disapproval. Fr. De Lamberville boldly invited her to come to pray at the chapel, an invitation that she longed to heed. It was the prompting she needed. Many of the elders and other chiefs of the town came to attend prayers at the chapel, as well, so for Tekakwitha to join in was by now what the majority of the villagers did, even if they just wanted to observe.[1]

The Jesuits wanted to be completely sure that a prospective convert understood the faith before administering the sacrament of baptism. It was considered more damning to have received the truth and later reject it than to have never received it in the first place, so the Jesuits wanted to be certain that a potential convert had every determination to remain a Christian. The only time the Jesuits baptized people on the spot was if someone were near death. They baptized many dying babies and elderly, but up until recently, it was a rare occasion in the Mohawk villages to baptize an adult. Adults understood the implications of converting, and many were not willing to disrupt the tribe and be looked upon as a traitor.

It is not hard to imagine the concern of the elders and medicine men over the introduction of a new religion into their established system of belief. The Mohawks were saddened and angered when groups of their people left to follow a new faith and subsequently left the tribe for the mission in Canada. Those left behind felt abandoned and vulnerable, because now they would need to replace those members through traditional warfare and capture. Survival depended on a population that could hunt and grow crops, and each capable person who left the tribe left a gap in productivity.

Luke 12:53 rings true in the situation of the Christians among the Mohawks: "They will be divided, father against son and son against father, mother against daughter and daughter against her mother, mother-in-law against her daughter-in-law and daughter-in-law against her mother-in-law." The traditional Iroquois considered those who converted and left traitors to their native way of life. And those that left went in search of freedom to live their new faith with those who accepted them.

Tekakwitha certainly knew that to be a Christian would put a wedge between herself and her tribe, but knowing her mother had been a Catholic surely nurtured her in the search for spiritual identity. She may have heard her mother recite the rosary each night in her native Algonquian language, kneeling in the longhouse as Tekakwitha lay on her mat nearby. And though the amount of instruction she may have had from her mother would have been limited—and she would have witnessed much more of her native customs and religion over the next decade—now the gateway was wide open to the road that would quench her search for a relationship with God himself.

The decision to become a Christian would bring disapproval from her family, but Tekakwitha did not find it difficult to be an outsider. Her life so far was one of being on the outside in many ways. She was one of the rare few who had survived smallpox, and there may also have been a certain amount of distance kept from them—not only because their faces were disfigured, but because, in their superstition, they believed some amount of evil might still be connected to them.

Another way that Tekakwitha was already different was the fact that she did not fully participate in the expected customs of the tribe because of her sensitivity to light. On sunny days it would have been impossible for Tekakwitha to join in the games children played or the ritual dances performed at festivals. Tekakwitha probably spent many hours of solitude and contemplation in the security of her longhouse, away from the boisterous and sometimes disturbing activities of the rest of her tribe. This ability to spend time alone is one characteristic that later led her to the mystical contemplation of the things of Christ and to learn the mysterious new faith at a rapid pace, as noted by her spiritual advisers.

But probably the strongest draw toward converting was that her mother had already paved the way for her: All who knew Tekakwitha also knew of her praying Christian mother. This may have given her the courage to make her way to the chapel for the first time. Tekakwitha must have obtained permission from her uncle to study the faith with Fr. De Lamberville and to attend the liturgies in the small chapel— permission that most likely was granted because of the agreement the Mohawks had made with the French to allow the Jesuit presence in their villages. If it were to be reported that the chief of the village was forbidding the Jesuits from teaching, then the Mohawks may have been in jeopardy of violating a peace treaty, something no one in the village would chance. So Tekakwitha became a pupil of the Jesuits.

KATERI, NEW CHRISTIAN

As soon as Tekakwitha was well enough to walk to the chapel to pray, it became her second home. If she wasn't at home, then everyone knew she was at the chapel praying.[2] It was not uncommon for the tribespeople to visit the chapel to observe the rituals of the Jesuits or to listen intently to them speak in the Iroquoian tongue using pictures of the Gospel story they had painted on birch bark. Most often, their presence was out of respect and curiosity—not for the intention of converting. As for Tekakwitha, however, she was fully engaged in all that they taught her, and with some spark of the Holy Spirit calling to her, she absorbed the truths of the Gospel at a rapid rate, memorizing all of her prayers.

After some months of instruction, Fr. De Lamberville made inquiries in the village regarding the moral life of Tekakwitha, to be sure that she was ready to become a Christian. One of her biographers wrote of what he found:

> Catherine had practiced her faith in such a manner, which her confessor admits she never once lessened from her original fervor. Everyone saw her extraordinary virtue, from the heathens to the faithful. The Christians saw her exactitude in obeying the rules of life. The Father had told her to go every day to the prayers of the morning and evening and every Sunday to assist Mass. The Father told her what she must avoid. These were the dream feasts, the dances and the other gatherings among the Natives that are contrary to purity. These general rules were good for the others, but Catherine had practiced all of this before her baptism.

The Father gave her some particular directions and regulated the prayers that she should say, as well as the practices of virtue to embrace. Catherine had such vigor to live in this manner.[3]

Once Fr. De Lamberville had learned that all in the village spoke well of her character, he determined she was ready for baptism along with two others and set the date for the special Feast of Easter day 1676.[4]

No doubt, Fr. De Lamberville was filled with satisfaction, assured that she was ready by her unwavering devotion and her steadfast conduct. Joyfully Tekakwitha awaited the day she could become a full follower of Christ. She was in love with him already and could hardly contain the excitement she felt as she counted the days until Easter. During the time of Lent that led up to her big day, she participated in the Catholic custom of the Stations of the Cross, where the Passion of Christ is commemorated. The story of Christ's suffering made a deep impact on her. She was able to enter into to his sufferings through her contemplation of it, and she was deeply moved by her own sin as the cause of his suffering. This deep sorrow for her sin and the sin of her people would grow in intensity as she grew closer to Jesus.

Fr. De Lamberville chose the name Catherine as the baptismal name for Tekakwitha, after St. Catherine of Siena, a perfect patron because their lives of consecration to Christ would have similar paths. Catherine was pronounced more like "Kateri" in Iroquoian and so her name comes down to us in this form.

On the April day, the walls and floors of the bark chapel were covered with pelts of beaver, bear, and wildcat in anticipation of the wonderful event about to take place with the baptism of Tekakwitha and two others. All the Christians who could attend came dressed in fancy outfits adorned with beads and belts of wampum. A children's choir started by Fr. Boniface added their angelic voices to the celebration.

Tekakwitha was clothed in a white garment, as baptismal candidates wear customarily. Within the church, she professed her faith, reciting the Creed and the Our Father on her knees. Then Fr. De Lamberville baptized her in the name of the Father, Son, and Holy Spirit, pouring the cleansing water over her forehead. She stood to her feet, eager and joyful to embrace the faith of the Church and renounce anything evil and not of God.

Up to this point, Kateri had been a rather obscure member of the tribe, known only because she was the niece of one of the chiefs. Within her longhouse she was much appreciated for her industrious contributions, but within the village of over five hundred people, she may have been recognized only as the girl who wore a blanket over her head. Once she took on the public commitment to be a Christian, however, she began to be singled out and ridiculed for her Christian practice, even by children who pointed at her as she walked by and called her a Christian as though the word were a curse.

Her aunts were especially perturbed with her firm commitment to observe Sundays and holy days, accusing her of being lazy because she would not work in the fields as all the other women did. Some sources say that her aunts were also Christians, but they did not hold the same fervor as Kateri in keeping the sabbath holy. They made it a point not to let her have food on the days that she did not work in the fields, hoping to force her to give up her Sunday and holy day observances.

They also encouraged others to harass her by following after her on her way to St. Peter's chapel, pretending to be drunk and throwing stones at her. This did not deter her in the least because her fervor to pray the rosary with the other Christians filled her with such joy. The Christians sang together as well, blending their voices in hymns between decades of the rosary. The harsh treatment of her aunts did not deter her from serving the family with kindness and docility.

On one occasion, her uncle even arranged to have a young man enter the longhouse brandishing a hatchet in an attempt to get Kateri to renounce her new faith, but, undeterred, she refused to be frightened by this threatening youth. She sat docilely on the floor of the longhouse with her head bowed, ignoring his antics. Finally he ran from the longhouse as though chased away by the spirit of peace she exuded.

The opposition from her tribe could not stop Kateri from her deep devotion and spiritual practices, so they began to attack her morality, twisting her words so she could be accused of impurity. During the hunting season, Kateri left the village with her aunts to accompany her uncle as he hunted. These excursions could last several days or weeks, and the group would set up a temporary camp out in the forest to use as a base. Kateri did not like being away from the village where she could have access to the chapel for prayer, but nevertheless, she continued her devotions by finding a quiet spot to kneel before a makeshift wooden cross. Several other hunters were also in their company, and in the course of the trip, Kateri's words were misinterpreted by one of her aunts to mean that Kateri was soliciting her husband. This was something totally out of character for Kateri, who avoided this type of male contact completely, unlike many of the other women in the village. As soon as they returned to Caughnawaga, the angry woman went immediately to Fr. De Lamberville to accuse Kateri of inappropriate conduct. Though Fr. De Lamberville thought it unlikely, he investigated the situation nevertheless, finding her innocent.

On several occasions, Kateri came to Fr. De Lamberville, disheartened by the harsh treatment from her aunts. He was greatly impressed with her ability to withstand the pressures from her longhouse, as she continued in humility to serve them and yet consistently attend prayers and Mass. He recommended that she go to the Mission at Sault St.

Louis, where the Great Mohawk had gone the previous year with his wife and several other Christians from Caughnawaga. Tekakwitha knew that she would be free to practice her faith unhindered there. Those at the Sault, as it was called, had agreed to ban polygamy, drunkenness, and superstition—three big issues that Christians had to confront on a daily basis in Mohawk territory. She gave the idea great consideration and surely her heart longed to be among others with the same desire to pray and who observed the sabbath. However, the disapproval from her uncle about the idea of leaving her longhouse must have weighed heavily on her mind.

THE SAULT

Word of Kateri's conversion had spread to the Sault, where Kateri's older sister and husband now lived. Her sister was no doubt elated and wished for Kateri to join her at the Sault. She sent her husband along with Hot Ashes, a chief convert from the Oneida, and a Huron convert to escort Kateri to the Sault and to see if there were any other converts wishing to make the journey.

Upon the arrival of the envoy, news spread of their coming and a crowd of curious people, including Kateri, went to Fr. De Lamberville's longhouse to listen to Hot Ashes speak about the joy of living at the Sault. Kateri's uncle was not among those listening in the crowd because he had gone to the Dutch settlement of Schenectady to do some trading. By this time in history, the British had captured the Dutch settlements and the area was renamed New York Province rather than New Amsterdam; Fort Orange was now Albany.

Once the crowd realized what Hot Ashes had come to say, they dispersed, disinterested in his offer, except for Kateri who was deeply moved by his appeal. Without her uncle's presence, it made it easier for Kateri to linger and learn all she could. With determination, she returned to her longhouse and made her wish to go to the Sault known. Her aunts did not object to her leaving, but she knew that her uncle would be adamantly against it.

Kateri's brother-in-law met her in secret to tell her that it was her sister who had sent them to get her. Delighted and energized to learn of this, Kateri determined that only death would stop her from leaving with them to go to the Sault. He explained the plan: Hot Ashes would continue on to preach at other villages of the Iroquois, leaving his spot in the canoe for Kateri to leave with her brother-in-law and the Huron.

Kateri was no doubt filled with anxiety as she secured the letters of recommendation from Fr. De Lamberville and put them into the satchel she would bring with her on her flight to New France. As she hurried down to the river with her brother-in-law and the Huron, she remembered his encouraging words to place her trust in God. She was on her way to a new life where her zeal for Christ could flourish. The long journey would carry them for several days of rigorous travel over land, lake, and river. But first, they needed to be vigilant, as surely Kateri's sudden disappearance would cause a commotion. Indeed, her uncle was notified, and he, knowing the trails that led to the north, loaded his gun and went in pursuit of the fugitives.

Kateri's brother-in-law had gone into Schenectady to buy some food and had actually crossed paths with Kateri's uncle, but somehow managed to go unrecognized. Meanwhile, Kateri and the Huron lay hidden among some tree branches and waited for Kateri's brother-in-law to return. They did not see her uncle again as the three continued on through the fall foliage toward Kateri's new home on the south bank of the St. Lawrence River. The mission was originally located outside the French settlement of La Prairie and had just relocated recently to Sault St. Louis, partly to find better farmland and partly to get away from the liquor trade that caused Native Americans struggling to be free of the grip of alcohol to stray from their conviction to avoid it. Sault St. Louis had a small chapel named St. Francis Xavier, which would soon welcome Kateri and become a place around which her new life would revolve.

The name of her new home, the Sault, was actually the French word for her old town of Caughnawaga, both meaning "by the rapids." The Native Americans referred to their village as Kanawake, an alternate spelling of Caughnawaga.

The day she first stepped into the Kanawake, Kateri's heart filled with elation. There she was reunited with her sister and was welcomed into her longhouse as a member. She also was reunited with Anastasia, the older woman who had known Kateri's mother and had known Kateri all her life. She embraced Kateri like her own daughter and was given the happy task of instructing Kateri in the faith. Kateri never tired of hearing stories from the Bible and of the saints. Like a sponge, she now could absorb not only the stories but the concepts of the faith. Her motivation to implement whatever she learned was noticed by everyone and was one thing that set her on the course to sainthood.

Kateri was also overjoyed to be under the spiritual council of three priests in residence at the time: Fr. Fremin, whom she had entertained in her uncle's longhouse ten years previous; Fr. Pierre Cholenec, who would become her spiritual adviser and official biographer; and Fr. Claude Chauchetiere, who had only come to New France four months prior. Fr. Chauchetiere would be greatly impressed by Kateri, and he too later wrote a story of her life.

Fr. Fremin surely recalled the moment he had met Kateri on his first mission to the Iroquois, when he stopped in Caughnawaga and had stayed in Kateri's longhouse. There he had made his first Mohawk convert, the woman dying from a scalp wound. There he had worked hard to start the mission at Tionondogen, where the battle against alcohol seemed almost insurmountable. Fr. Fremin must have looked fondly upon Kateri, the eager young Christian, so full of excitement to be at the Sault. Here was a young woman now a part of the Sault, partly as a result of the mission work he had undertaken in her homeland.

The Sault was built on a bluff overlooking a stretch of rapids that churned the St. Lawrence River and filled the silence of the surrounding woods with the sound of its mighty rushing. The chapel and residences of the Jesuits were surrounded by strong wooden walls with twenty longhouses for the Native Americans built just beyond the church compound.[5] Life in the longhouses and surrounding fields—food, clothing, hunting, and farming—went on much as it did back in Caughnawaga, but the spiritual dimension of it revolved around the Church rather than the dreams and superstitions on which they all had been raised.

Fr. Cholenec received the letters from Fr. De Lamberville, observing the frail young maiden wrapped in a crimson blanket with her beaming expression across her scarred face. The words of Fr. De Lamberville urged him to take charge of Kateri's spiritual direction. "It is a treasure which we are giving you, as you will soon realize. Guard it well and make it bear fruit for the glory of God and the salvation of a soul which is certainly very dear to him."[6]

Chapter Five

LIFE AT KANAWAKE: LIVING THE SACRAMENTS
1677–1679

Many Jesuit sources mention how much the Sault (Kanawake) was similar to the early church right after Christ's resurrection, when all lived together and shared what they had, so filled with zeal and joy that they could never cease praying or sharing the teachings of Christ and his disciples.[1] This was the atmosphere of the mission, united to pray and attempting to glorify Christ in their every action. A sense of expectancy about what wonderful things may happen, prompted by the Holy Spirit, filled the hearts of both the Christians and those neophytes receiving instruction, who were awaiting the day they would be ready for baptism and able to join fully in the sacraments. The hearts of these Native Americans were open to receive all that they could hold of Catholic teaching and practice. They enthusiastically engaged in songs, prayers, and devotions, and they embraced each new teaching with fervor. The Jesuits marveled at the ardor of these new converts in contrast to Catholic practice among the Europeans of the day. The Native Americans at Kanawake could possibly have been one of the most devout groups of Christians to have ever lived in community.

For all of her life, Kateri had lived on the fringe, never participating fully in the life of those who surrounded her. As a child up until the time the Jesuits built the mission of St. Peter near her village, she did not venture outside her longhouse except for work. Following her conversion, she was again on the fringe for participating in the spiritual life of the Christians. But now at Kanawake, she fit in perfectly and fell immediately into the rhythm of the mission.

There was no more disapproval for attending prayers or keeping the sabbath. Here she freely attended Mass on Sundays at dawn and then again at 8:00 A.M., remaining in the chapel between Masses to pray her rosary, which she carried with her everywhere, in her hand or around her neck. She went to confession every Saturday—which she would prepare for by hitting her shoulders with large branches for penance, while weeping for her sins. In confession, she grieved with sighs and sobs for what she considered were her detestable sins. She didn't want anything to separate her from God.

On weekdays, she attended morning and evening prayers, and, after working with the others for the day, she would return at once to the chapel to continue her vigil of prayer before the Blessed Sacrament on display in the silver monstrance on the altar in the chapel of St. Francis Xavier. As she knelt before the Blessed Sacrament, at times trance-like for several hours, she prayed not so much with her voice as with her eyes, which were often filled with tears.

Though she grieved for her sins and those of her people, she was also a pleasant and joyful person who enjoyed making others laugh.[2] She expressed no thought of reprimand or derogatory comment, but wanted to continue her spiritual growth at all times. While occupied in the longhouse, she liked to sing devotional hymns with the others or initiate discussions about stories from the lives of the saints or discuss a sermon. She kept in the company of Anastasia whenever she could, constantly asking to learn more from her because she had been a Christian for many years and knew many stories of the saints.

As much as Kateri liked to spend time with devout Christians, she also desired alone time to be in conversation with Christ in prayer. The chapel of St. Francis Xavier became one of her favorite spots. A belt of wampum five feet long was suspended from the ceiling beams over the altar within the chapel. It was a gift from a sister mission of Huron Christians located at Loretto near Quebec, who wanted to exhort their brothers and sisters to sincerely follow the faith. In the center of the belt was a white cross, and extending to its right and left were patterns, white against the purple background, that represented the straight path of the Ten Commandments and the Catholic faith that leads to heaven and the crooked path of superstition and sin that leads to hell.

The Hurons wanted to encourage the Iroquois to fight against the temptations that may lure them from the faith, and they also wished for them to build a permanent chapel.[3] The message of the belt helped to remind the faithful to persevere on the good road, a goal that Kateri strove toward along with the others at Kanawake. The Jesuits had illustrated to them during their instructions with words and paintings the consequences of going down the road leading to hell. The most common native practices that led down the wrong road were alcohol, superstition, and immorality. To counteract these temptations, the natives on the mission tried as strictly as they could to attend prayers and to avoid influences from the outside.

Though Kateri had been baptized, she had not yet received the sacrament of Holy Communion. This was the next step in her journey, one she greatly anticipated. For the converts, another period of instruction followed baptism to ensure that the new Christian fully understood the sacrament in which the Body and Blood of Christ were consumed. The Native Americans did understand—in some ways more than modern Christians—how the eating of a person's flesh and drinking of their blood imparts their life into the receiver. The reason that the Iroquois ate strong warriors that they had killed was because they believed the strength of the warrior would then be passed on to them. It was not difficult for converts to understand how partaking of the Body and Blood of Christ would impart his grace and nature into their lives.

As Christmas approached, Kateri's spiritual adviser, Fr. Cholenec, thought it would be appropriate for Kateri to receive Communion on Christmas Day, only two months after her arrival at Kanawake. It was evident to all that Kateri understood the mystery of the sacrament of the Eucharist. She perceived that the reception of Holy Communion brought her to a close identification with Christ. At this time in history, Pope Pius X had not yet declared that the laity should go to Communion frequently, so reception of the Eucharist was not a common practice at Kanawake (although Mass attendance was).

Christmas was celebrated with all the excitement of today, but not because of the exchanging of gifts—rather over the mystery of the Incarnation, that God became man. The infant Jesus in the manger scene was central in the chapel, and everyone came to gaze upon him. The chapel was decorated with furs, feathers, and woven tapestries to mark the holy day. During the Mass, Kateri took her turn at the Communion rail and received Jesus into her body for the first time. This occasion brought her closer to Christ, and she showed her gratitude by redoubling her efforts to love him through even more fervent prayer and penance.

The next occasion in which she could receive Holy Communion was the feast of Easter, one year after her baptism. As she had the previous year, she participated in the awe-filled days of Holy Week. On Good Friday, when the cross was displayed for veneration, Kateri approached it to kneel before it with kisses and sobs, and she followed a renewed ardor to suffer with Christ.[4] The Iroquois were not embarrassed to express their feelings with gestures and loud noises. In Native American upbringing, it was natural to express deep feelings, both of joy and of sorrow, and Kateri expressed her remorse for the death of Christ with deep emotion.

Due to the expertise of the Jesuits in language, the Creed, parts of the Mass, prayers, and devotions had been translated into Iroquoian so the Natives could better participate. Music also was translated from the Latin and sung by choirs and by all. The Native Americans had a love and talent for music, since it had always been a part of their ceremonies and a way to express thanks to the spirits. These beautiful Christian songs continued to be sung for 350 years at Kanawake.[5]

DEEP DEVOTION: THE HOLY FAMILY ASSOCIATION

A few years earlier, a group called The Holy Family Association had been formed in New France. It encouraged women and mothers to imitate St. Mary, men and fathers to imitate St. Joseph, and children to imitate Christ, the obedient Son. A chapter of this organization had also begun at Kanawake a few years prior to Kateri's arrival, and only those who were the most devout in their faith were invited to be part of it. Anastasia, Kateri's instructress, belonged to the Holy Family Association. For many years, Anastasia had labored successfully in her Christian practice and was respected for her wisdom and knowledge. This was the typical member of the Association, who others admired for their examples of faith.

Kateri followed Anastasia all about, eagerly asking questions. Each time Kateri learned of something new, she did all she could to practice it. Her zeal for the faith was the reason Kateri, too, was chosen to be a member of the Holy Family Association.[6] It was said that those who were members of the Association were considered as holy as the saints by the residents of Kanawake.[7] The Association met at one o'clock on Sunday afternoons for prayer and singing of the psalms and the *Ave Maria*. The intent of the group was not only to practice their devotions and prayers but to be an example to the others and encourage them and instruct them to go deeper in faith. They also were to safeguard the community from outside pressures of alcohol and immorality.

Kateri was filled with thanksgiving for her new life at Kanawake—a type of earthly paradise compared to the culture of her native land.[8] Kateri's capacity for thankfulness had been fostered in her since her youth. It was a concept deeply embedded into the Iroquois, as reflected in every festival and council meeting when a thanksgiving address is given at the beginning. The Iroquois believed that the Sky Holder, who had fashioned humankind, had instilled into humans the need to express gratitude the moment they met one another and, regardless of the circumstances, to be thankful for one another. Even in the worst of circumstances, one could always be thankful for Mother Earth and all her bounty.[9]

Oral tradition had played a large role in Kateri's life growing up, as many an evening long tales were dramatically told around the fire. Because of this sort of training, Kateri and the other Native Americans were able to absorb and easily retain the new stories from the faith— and some of the traditional stories were like groundwork in helping bridge some Catholic teachings.

Two native stories with which Kateri would have been very familiar were the Iroquois creation story and the story of the Great Peacemaker, both stories involving an unmarried woman. As she learned about St. Mary from the Jesuits, these traditional stories most certainly came to mind, especially the concept of the virgin birth, since women in both of these stories conceived without knowing a man. Kateri developed a deep devotion to the Blessed Mother, influenced surely by the Holy Family Association that promoted the imitation of St. Mary and certainly the rosary.

In the Iroquois creation story, a woman falls through a hole in the sky and lands on a turtle, upon which animals pile mud until it forms the land. The Sky Woman gives birth to a girl who grows up and becomes pregnant when a man lays two arrows beside her, after which she has twin sons, one who was good and helped corn, tobacco, and fruit to grow, and the other who was bad and created weeds and pests. Later the Sky Holder makes five pairs of people who then form the tribes of the Iroquois League.[10]

The story of the Great Peacemaker is very interesting in that nearly all Native American tribes have some form of this story, in which a messiah-type man comes to teach people how to live uprightly. In the Iroquois version of this story, the Great Peacemaker was born of a virgin girl who had not yet gone through the traditional rite of passage of puberty, which included living alone in a hut in the woods for the duration of the menstrual cycle. Women continued to live alone in the woods each time they had a cycle, so Kateri would also have spent time in this way for this same reason.

The virgin in the Peacemaker story becomes pregnant, much to the dismay of her mother, who hides her away until the child is born. The grandmother tries to kill the baby, but realizes that a great destiny is upon him because of his great powers. When he grows up, he unites the Iroquois tribes with the help of Hiawatha and teaches them how to live in peace. This story easily translated into the virgin birth of Christ, who brought peace to the whole world. The Native Americans believed in Christ, as they learned the full revelation of him when the Jesuits explained the Gospel.

In addition to her devotional life at the mission, Kateri eagerly worked to gather bundles of firewood for the cook fires, which was her assigned task. Though still affected by a limp from the injury she had sustained a few years back, Kateri diligently did her share of the work, never complaining. Gathering firewood brought her great joy, as the work was done in solitude and she could continue her revelry of prayer and meditating upon the tenets of the faith.

However, on one occasion as she was felling a tree with her hatchet, she miscalculated, and the tree began to fall on her. She managed to dodge the main trunk, but a branch hit her in the head, causing her to be knocked unconscious. Her worried companions, Anastasia among them, pulled her limp body from beneath the branches and began to call out her name. Suddenly Kateri's eyes flew open, and she exclaimed, "O Jesus, I thank you for having rescued me from danger." Her relieved companions carried her home, though she protested that she was well enough to work. This occasion became another turning point for Kateri. She saw it as a message from God that she had been allowed to live longer in order to do penance for sin.[11]

Sacrifice and Self-Denial

The practice among the Christians at Kanawake included forms of penance that today we would consider very extreme, but physical penance was something practiced and admired by the Church in general in the seventeenth century with the aid of iron girdles, bands with spikes on the inside that were worn around the waist. In our way of thinking today, we find it hard to comprehend that God would be pleased by us abusing our bodies, but during the Middle Ages until the modern era, austerity and asceticism were often what divided the average person from the person bound for sainthood.

In the case of St. Catherine of Siena, the baptismal namesake of Kateri, we can read about her life of asceticism and wonder if some of the things she did were beyond what God would expect of anyone. One particular practice of St. Catherine's, which is very difficult to imagine today in our sanitary world, is, as she cared for lepers, she would take the water from which she washed their sores and drink it. For us it is hard to comprehend, but for the people of her day, this was a supreme sacrifice. For her, it brought her closer to Christ because she saw her action as an act of love toward Christ.

It was known that the Great Mohawk at Kanawake wore iron girdles on Fridays and holy days as a form of penance.[12] The Jesuits supplied the girdles to the Natives who wished to use them. The women of the village were also very fervent with penance and did many things to chastise themselves, such as standing in the icy river while reciting the rosary or beating their backs until bloody with switches.

The Jesuits tried to curb excessive penance, but the Natives often did these acts in the woods beyond the eyes of their spiritual advisers. Kateri also began to engage in many forms of penance. At times, she walked barefoot in the snow for long distances while praying. Fasting, physical penance, and sleep deprivation all contributed to Kateri's fragile health, but regardless of her exhaustion, she would rise at 4:00 A.M. with the ringing of the mission bell and return home from prayers as the last one in the evening, many times with little to eat. She did this out of her own desire to suffer with Christ and to show him her sincerity.

From the very earliest years of an Iroquois's life, the toughening of the body in order to endure was highly important. Being able to physically withstand cold, hunger, and pain would strengthen them in order to survive whatever may come along. In the spiritual realm, the Native Americans who embraced Christianity saw physical endurance as a way to bring themselves closer to God, for in the Native American way of thinking, there is no separation between the physical and the spiritual. The rituals of the False Face medicine society were meant to drive away the bad spirits that affected *both* the mind and the body. The practice of penance for the Native American Christians, then, was connected to endurance, and physically buffeting themselves made their faith become stronger because a body that could endure also meant a strengthening of the spirit over evil.

Some examples of endurance training show us how tough they were. Immediately after baby boys were born, they were plunged into a river and held there for several seconds, no matter how cold the water. That was done to make them brave hunters.[13] Part of the Iroquois's upbringing included training to endure the torture of burning without crying out, an essential skill should they be captured by an enemy. Our modern day game of lacrosse originated among the Iroquois as a prewar game to build stamina and to endure blows from sticks and balls hurled toward them. Though women did not train for warfare, they too learned to withstand the tests of the elements, cold, fire, and hunger.

Fasting among the Christians was also a common discipline. A Dutch observer had commented on the eating habits of the Iroquois in this way: "They do not observe customary or fixed meal times as our people usually do and judge it best to eat when they are hungry. They have tremendous control over their appetites, stomachs and bodies, so that they can get by with very little for two, three, or four days. When supplies are ample once again, they will quickly make up for the loss or delay, yet this does not upset their stomachs or make them ill. Though good eaters they are not gluttons."[14]

When boys and girls reached puberty, they were sent off on their own for a period of time to fast. Fasting was a typical method for the

Iroquois to tap into the spiritual world. While fasting, they hoped to receive a vision from the spirits to direct their decision in a certain matter. For the Catholic, the use of fasting is also a means of bringing oneself more closely in tune with the spiritual dimension, because in the process of denying the body of its wants, the mind and soul become more attuned to the spirit of God. With the predisposition of the Iroquois Christians to fast, it became a natural expression among them.

When Kateri was alone in the forest, she often found ways to mortify herself, believing it benefited her spiritual growth. She also fasted often and avoided being in the longhouse while the food was cooking. If she did eat, she mixed her sagamite with ashes so it wasn't pleasurable, and in this way she could deny herself in order to grow closer to Christ. She took pains to do these things without being noticed.

Among the young women that Kateri knew, she became very close to one named Mary Theresa, a twenty-eight-year-old widow. They met as both of them eagerly watched the construction of a new church on the compound—one much bigger than the humble chapel they currently used. The new church would be sixty feet long and would have four bells to call the faithful to prayers with melodious harmonies. Kateri's deep faith influenced Mary Theresa to reform her ways, and the two of them became inseparable.

Mary Theresa was deeply sorry for a grave sin she had committed during the hunt on which her husband had died of an illness. She and her nephew were left as part of a band of fifteen Iroquois who became stranded in the forest because they had not found anything to eat. Eventually, the group resorted to killing and eating three of the band in order to stay alive. Mary Theresa was deeply grieved that she had not tried to stop the group from killing the others. For this and for what she saw as her weak faith, she did penance by hitting herself. Kateri confided in her that she too disciplined herself in that manner, sometimes to the point of bleeding.

The bond between the two women led to the practice of severe penance together. In secret, they would go to a trader's hut that was empty, and there they would take turns whipping one another's backs with switches. They accelerated their discipline until they reached one thousand strikes, leaving them both exhausted and bloody, yet with a feeling of exhilaration. They stole away to perform these acts before they would go to confession. They encouraged one another to endure burning coals between their toes, an idea that Mary Theresa nearly shrank from, but Kateri tried, keeping the ember in place as she recited an entire rosary. There were many excesses that other women performed, as well. The Jesuits were unaware of what was going on, as all those involved in such things kept them a secret, most likely knowing that the priests would make them stop.

Each year in the winter the Iroquois would go on a big hunt when tracking animals in the snow made it easier to find their prey. Since the women were not able to farm at this time, they accompanied the hunters to prepare the animals that were killed and to maintain daily camp life in their temporary shelters. Kateri accompanied her sister and brother-in-law, along with several others, into the woods. She found it difficult to be away from St. Francis Xavier chapel, and she made a prayer shrine near a stream, where she carved a cross into a tree trunk. She would pray there at the times she knew the priests were saying Mass back at Kanawake.

An event that left Kateri heartbroken occurred on this trip and led her to never want to leave the mission on a hunting trip again. One of the devout women of Kanawake, who at the time did not know Kateri very well, became suspicious of her husband's conduct with Kateri. One night, her husband returned exhausted from the hunt and crept into the sleeping area in the dark, finding the first spot he could find open, which happened to be next to Kateri. In the morning light, the woman noticed where her husband had ended up and was not pleased about it.

Later, he asked Kateri to help him finish some work on his canoe, knowing that Kateri was capable of the work and always willing to help. To his wife, however, this confirmed her suspicions. She said nothing until they returned to Kanawake, when she went directly to Fr. Fremin to report the incident. Fr. Cholenec, being assigned as Kateri's spiritual adviser, took it upon himself to further investigate the accusation against Kateri by asking her if she had been involved with this man, who also was a very upright Christian. Kateri calmly replied that she would do nothing of the sort. Believing her by her quiet manner, Fr. Cholenec pursued the matter no further; however, the seeds of doubt sewn among those to whom the woman confided continued to circulate.

It broke Kateri's heart to be suspected of something so far from the truth, but she bore the reproach with her continued virtue and kindness, never speaking ill of her accuser. Fr. Chauchetiere later wrote that he realized during one of his teaching sessions that Kateri was so innocent of slandering anyone because she did not even understand the meaning of the concept since it was so foreign to her.

BRIDE OF CHRIST

Fr. Cholenec allowed Kateri to travel the short distance to Ville-Marie, now Montreal, with Mary Theresa, probably to do some trading of their handiwork with the French settlers. The beadwork sewn onto purses had become a popular trade item. The town of about six hundred residents was located across the St. Lawrence from Kanawake. There was the stone chapel of Notre-Dame-de-Bon-Secours, built for pilgrims at the urging of Marguerite Bourgeoys. She has since become a saint for founding the Congregation of Notre Dame, where she labored to educate and care for the poor and the Native Americans. She was also one of the founding members of the Holy Family Association.

After stopping to pray in the chapel, Kateri and Mary Theresa visited the Hotel Dieu, where Kateri saw for the first time women who were celibate—the Sisters Hospitallers of St. Joseph, who were nurses at the hospital. Deeply intrigued by their communal life, Kateri immediately began to dream of living in a similar situation with Mary Theresa and other friends who would want to join her in such a venture.

When she and Mary Theresa returned to Kanawake, Marie Skarichions, an older Christian woman, joined them in their new plan to found their own religious community. They scanned the surrounding area for a suitable location, choosing Heron Island amidst the churning rapids as a likely spot. With high hopes, Kateri approached Fr. Fremin with her idea, but he dismissed the notion with a chuckle, knowing full well how difficult that would be. To start an order of nuns, there would need to be a base of support, and at this young stage of the mission, the concept of supporting a group of young women was out of the question, not to mention dangerous. They would be unprotected from raiding Iroquois who would not hesitate to capture them and bring them back to Iroquois territory. The women did not question Fr. Fremin's decision; however, the wish to stay a virgin remained a high priority for Kateri.

After Anastasia pointed out to Kateri that perhaps she was still showing vanity by wearing ornaments about her neck and hair and wearing red clothing, Kateri quickly removed these items from her wardrobe and exchanged her red blanket for a simple blue one.[15] She was remorseful for her vanity and confessed this as a sin, with tears. She had no intention of catching a man's eye with ornaments or attractive clothing.

Kateri observed how priests and nuns did not marry, and for them it was a good thing. So why then would it be necessary for her to marry? She had a natural inclination to be single—and the spiritual desire to be united only to Christ as her spouse, even though she had not been instructed in this way. She pressed Fr. Fremin for more information, sensing that her advisers were not sharing everything they knew with her about this matter of celibacy. What finally drove her to beg Fr. Cholenec for help was a threatening attempt by her sister to force Kateri to get married.

Similar to what had occurred in Caughnawaga when her aunts tried to trick her into marriage with a young warrior, now her sister in Kanawake was following the same bent for the same reason. A woman should have a man who could provide meat for food, hides for clothing, and a number of other things necessary for day-to-day life. Kateri's sister saw no reason why Kateri should continue to be a drain on her and her husband for her livelihood, and since Kateri was such a model of virtue, what single Christian man would not want her as his wife? She had no idea how firmly Kateri had already decided in her own heart to remain unmarried.

One day Kateri had to listen to a long speech from her sister, imploring her to choose a husband in order to bring provisions to the longhouse. She tried to reason with Kateri by saying her husband was not getting any younger and if some misfortune should occur, what would happen then? To secure her future, she needed to find a husband.[16] Kateri agreed to think about her sister's proposal. She in no way wanted to be a burden to her sister or to displease her, but what she was asking was impossible in Kateri's mind.

Her only recourse was to go to Fr. Cholenec and ask for his help. She poured out her heart to him, telling him that she did not wish to marry and that she would not be a burden to anyone because she could sew items that could be traded among the European settlers. Fr. Cholenec was swayed by her sincerity and shared more details with her about those who took vows of celibacy like the nuns at Ville-Marie. In Kateri's culture, however, it was not customary to remain unmarried, and he asked her to think the matter over carefully. He did tell her however that it should be her free choice whether she marry or not.

She told him, "I cannot give in to this. I dislike men and have the utmost aversion to marriage."[17] Her dark eyes must have pooled with tears.

"Kateri, you cannot take this idea lightly. Your sister cares about your welfare and you should think about what she has explained to you," Fr. Cholenec said gently.

"I am not afraid of the poverty with which they threaten me; it takes so little to provide for the needs of this temporary life that my work will be enough to take care of it, and I can surely find a few rags to wear," she declared.[18]

"Come back after you have thought about it thoroughly," Fr. Cholenec said kindly as Kateri left to go home.

The moment Kateri stepped into the door, her sister asked if she had made up her mind. Kateri's decision had been made long ago, and now she boldly spoke to her sister about it. She told her sister that she would not marry nor would she be a burden to her. She would not be destitute because she would work for her own keep. Her sister began to dispute this, bewildered that any girl would have such an idea as remaining single. Among the Christians, marriage to one's spouse for life was a virtue that was highly promoted, since in the Native American way of life, marriages could be dissolved very easily and multiple marriages were common. A sacramental marriage would be a wonderful Christian example, so it was confusing to think that Kateri completely refused the idea.

Kateri wanted to be free to choose her spiritual path, and she had been strongly drawn to celibacy long before she knew it was an option in her new faith. Just as she had been able to grow up avoiding many superstitious practices of her people, she had also been able to remain a virgin, something she innately saw as important. She wanted to commit herself to a life of devotion to Christ and only to him.

Her sister was concerned that Kateri would be tempted to sin. Kateri countered with words of resolve saying she would trust in God to help her resist sin. Then she begged her sister not to press her any more about the issue. In her mind, it was settled forever: She would never marry. It was not often that Kateri spoke so adamantly, so her sister did not speak to her about it again. However, she did convince Anastasia to back her in this request, and so Anastasia too tried to explain to Kateri the necessity of a young woman to get married, to no avail.

"Just be sure you won't regret this decision someday," Anastasia finally said.

After this episode, she returned again to Fr. Cholenec to complain about her sister and Anastasia. She told him firmly that she wanted to take a vow of virginity. Fr. Cholenec was moved by her request. This was something very unusual, since she had not been instructed in this way. The Catholic culture during this era highly esteemed those who took a vow of virginity because it closely identified the woman with the Virgin Mary. Virginity was a spiritual sign of purity and sinlessness, and a vow of virginity was a sign of total commitment to Christ as their only spouse. Celibacy in general allows a person to totally focus upon their relationship with Christ and not to be distracted with the needs of another, although this does not exclude the celibate person from loving and caring for others.

Fr. Cholenec asked Kateri to think seriously about taking such a vow. He needed time to discern what to do in this new situation as well, so he asked her to take three days to pray about it. She agreed, but in less than fifteen minutes she returned to tell him she had made this choice long ago and there was no reason to think or pray anymore about it. She told him that she was willing to live in poverty and would consider herself fortunate if she could live with Jesus Christ as her only spouse.

Fr. Cholenec was convinced by her words and laid the matter to rest with Anastasia and Kateri's sister. He told Kateri that neither he nor his fellow missionaries would ever abandon her or fail to provide for her if she chose to remain a virgin. Kateri's spirit was lifted to heights of joy. With gratitude, Kateri went her way, dreaming of the day she could officially express her deep commitment in a public vow.

On March 25, 1679, the feast of the Assumption, after receiving Holy Communion, Kateri professed her vow of virginity, renouncing the security that marriage could provide and giving herself to Christ's care. From this point on, Kateri found a certain independence and freedom in being obligated only to Christ. On that same day, Kateri consecrated herself to the Blessed Mother, taking her as her mother.

Chapter Six

PENANCE AND DEATH
1679–1680

An unprecedented period of time occurred during the summer of 1679 in which the people of Kanawake engaged in extreme and bloody penances. Their fervor and their ability to endure great pain without any sign of discomfort must have amazed the Jesuits. They were pleased that their converts were so grieved by their past lives, but the Jesuits found it difficult to monitor what was happening, and they did not know the extent of what Kateri and Mary Theresa were doing until after Kateri's health was irreversibly affected.

Though the Native Americans saw these acts as offerings of themselves, their intensity had gotten out of control. In vain, Fr. Fremin and Fr. Cholenec tried to teach them moderate forms of penance, but those methods would not do in the eyes of these converts whose physical expression of faith far outdid any other group of its time.

Kateri's ascetic practices were her way of giving herself to her spouse, Jesus. Kateri expressed her self-denial, based on both the beliefs of her native people and the Catholic faith, in order to bring herself into a deeper realm of heightened sensitivity. Her actions were motivated by an intense desire to please Christ, and, in her mind, the more severe the practice, the deeper the sacrifice she was making. The Gospel does ask us all to deny ourselves, pick up our cross, and follow Christ, and the way in which an ascetic person practices the call to self-denial brings to him a type of spiritual fulfillment. Kateri reported to the priests on one occasion that, while scourging herself repeatedly in the dark, a bright light surrounded her and remained with her for a long time.[1] This type of experience often accompanies those who engage in severe penance, as they reach a place outside of the natural realm.

This is not the way for all people to carry out this request of Christ. However, for many centuries it was a practice of the Church that brought others to faith. During the fifth century, one amazing group of people was the *stylites*. They climbed poles and stood on top of them for years, denying themselves, and in this way witnessed to others of their total commitment to Christ. Throngs of people would seek them out in order to renew their faith, ask for healing, and repent of their sins. There was something about the intensity of the stylites' commitment that caused others to respond with spiritual hunger.

Two factors come into play in the relationship between the ascetic person and those who observe him. First, the ascetic is able to unite himself to Christ in a way unobtainable without severe self-denial, and second, those who witness the person's life are drawn to him with a spiritual hunger and then gain the grace of God through the suffering and sacrifice of the ascetic person. An effect similar to this comes upon those who are in the presence of holiness—and the responses hopefully lead to spiritual graces.

This began to prove true as people even outside of the village heard of Kateri's penance and came to see her. Kateri was surprised that anyone had learned of her practices. A couple came to her and asked what sort of thing they should do to please God, but, not wanting to act as a spiritual adviser, she referred them to the priests for counsel. A group of thirteen women surrounded Kateri and became known as Kateri's band. They met to exhort one another to holiness and to perform secret acts of kindness for the poor and sick of the village. They all refrained from wearing jewelry and busied themselves sewing, something they had learned from the French.

Each one of them was involved in some type of severe penance. One lashed herself four thousand times. Another cut herself from head to toe. Another stood in an icy stream so long that ice formed on her, and she slept in that condition on her mat in the longhouse. There were probably all sorts of other attempts like these that went unrecorded. We know of Kateri's penances because Mary Theresa eventually shared them with their spiritual adviser, Fr. Cholenec.

On one occasion, Kateri burned her leg with a brand from ankle to knee. Another time, she burned a hole in her foot with a burning coal. She began to get sick from the severity of her mortifications, but still she would not stop. She continued in her daily practice of prayer even on the coldest days, kneeling in the unheated chapel. Fr. Cholenec tried to send her home or warm her by the fire of his home, but she would return to kneel before the Blessed Sacrament.

Fr. Cholenec commented that because of "her extreme thirst for suffering," he gave Kateri an iron girdle to wear so she would not scourge herself so harshly.[2] She wore it a few times per week during her daily work of carrying bundles of wood, and on one occasion she slipped on the ice and fell down a hill, causing the spikes to dig deeply into her skin. Even then she did not stop working or remove the girdle until evening. Mary Theresa also wore the girdle on alternate days.

On one occasion, Kateri's band of women went to the cemetery to dig a grave for a family member, when their conversation turned to the Four Last Things: death, judgment, hell, and heaven, a common topic among those at Kanawake. In the course of the conversation, Kateri in jest pointed to a plot of land in the cemetery where she said she would be buried when her life on earth ended. Uncanny as it seems, it was the exact location that Fr. Cholenec would choose for her gravesite within the year.

As the winter passed, Kateri's health declined to the point that at times she could barely function. Mary Theresa attended her and was struck with the terror that perhaps she had contributed to her dear friend's condition. She went to Fr. Cholenec and disclosed all the details of Kateri's mortification, which they previously had hid from him. "We wanted to imitate the saints of God," Mary Theresa explained. Fr. Cholenec reproached her for the excesses but was still quite amazed at what these women endured. He instructed her and Kateri that penance was to be done in moderation, not in such excess that their health was compromised.

After this, Kateri's health improved somewhat until the season of Lent approached, and the fervor of severe penance began anew among Kateri's band. Kateri accompanied some women on a journey to the village of La Prairie in the bitter cold, and once again her health declined. It was about this time that Fr. Claude Chauchetiere became more involved in Kateri's life. He was assigned now to visit Kateri every day. He had not been a spiritual adviser to the Christians, but among other duties was given the task of teaching the children. He would teach catechism lessons to his charge of children in Kateri's presence. She begged him to return every day so she could hear more about the Bible.

As Lent progressed, Fr. Chauchetiere had a premonition that Kateri would die on the Wednesday of Holy Week.[3] As each day passed, he became more impressed with her eagerness to learn the faith and her ability to suffer so joyfully.

Sensing also that the day she would meet Jesus was approaching, Kateri felt compelled to perform some act of mortification. Since she was not allowed to beat herself or wear the girdle, she found another way. As she went to fetch firewood, she cut some thorns from a bush and snuck them into the house to put on her sleeping mat. For three days she slept on them, after which she was discovered by Mary Theresa, who could tell something was happening because she was growing weaker each day. Mary Theresa reproached her with concern, telling her she didn't have permission to do this.

Worried that she had sinned, Kateri went to Fr. Cholenec to tell him. He could see how weak and depleted she was from this last bout of mortification, and once again he ordered her to stop and to go immediately home to burn the thorns. However, from this point on she grew very sick, with severe vomiting and stomach pains and a persistent fever. She had to lie down, the least movement causing great pain, but she never complained. To her, her own suffering seemed nothing compared to what Christ suffered on the cross for the sins of the world.

As life went on around her with everyone else engaged in daily chores and prayers at the chapel, Kateri lay in the solitude of her house, using the time to pray the rosary, fingering each bead with sincerity and occasionally kissing a copper crucifix given to her by Fr. Cholenec.

Earthly Life Nearing Its End

On Palm Sunday, Fr. Cholenec realized that Kateri's death was fast approaching. Mary Theresa rarely left her best friend's side. On Tuesday as Fr. Cholenec knelt beside her, Kateri asked through her wracking pain if she would be allowed to do some form of penance, perhaps not to eat or drink for the day. He could not agree with her request, even though he knew she meant only to be as close to Jesus as she could during Passion Week. He told her God was pleased with her great love for him and would perhaps show her his love soon.[4] He could see that she was very close to that moment when she would be in the arms of Jesus. He promised to bring Kateri Holy Communion.

When others were sick, they were brought to the chapel on a board in order to receive Holy Communion, but Fr. Cholenec decided he would bring the sacrament to her in the longhouse, due to her specific circumstances. As Fr. Cholenec hurried away to prepare for this, Kateri turned to Mary Theresa and asked if she could borrow her beaded vest in order to be ready for this special occasion. The state of Kateri's poverty was such that she had no suitable clothing of her own. She had chosen this state by renouncing marriage, but as she had once told Fr. Cholenec, she found herself "fortunate to live in poverty and misery for [Christ's] love."[5]

We can better understand through the example of Kateri the joy to be found in poverty. The Scripture rings so true of Kateri in the Beatitude, "Blessed are the poor in spirit, for theirs is the kingdom of heaven" (Matthew 5:3). She was blessed on earth and in heaven in her total poverty. Although the Bible instructs us to feed the hungry and clothe the naked, it also tells us to be content in all things. Kateri was satisfied even if her needs were not met. She completely trusted Christ for her existence and did not spend her life worrying. Instead, she focused all her energy on how to love Christ in her simplicity. She did not feel that she was entitled to anything; rather, she embraced her poverty as an offering to Christ. It is a mystery to us how Kateri could rejoice in her poverty and in her bodily discomforts.

A crowd gathered in the longhouse as Fr. Cholenec returned from the chapel with the Blessed Sacrament, walking behind a cross bearer and two acolytes who carried lighted candles. The congregation began to recite a prayer of repentance before Fr. Cholenec raised the host for all to gaze upon. Then he placed the consecrated host upon Kateri's tongue. The onlookers surely must have sensed the sanctity of the moment when the dying Kateri, whom they all admired, received Jesus in the sacrament. When everyone left, Fr. Cholenec remained to do one last examination of Kateri's piety. It may have been a routine practice among the Jesuits to ask questions of the dying to be sure they were prepared, but Kateri was saddened that he even asked a question regarding her chastity. "No, no," she struggled to say. It was unthinkable for her to have ever compromised her virginity, especially since she had promised it to Jesus.

Fr. Cholenec asked her if she wanted the sacrament of Extreme Unction, which at that time was administered right at the moment of death. Today the sacrament is called the anointing of the sick and can be given to those who are sick but not necessarily at the point of death. Kateri felt she was not ready for Extreme Unction yet. After Fr. Cholenec left, realizing this might be their last time to see Kateri, throughout the day the villagers visited her to ask for her prayers or bits of advice. She exhorted them to persevere in penance and to live in harmony together.

All through the night, two of her companions who were also members of the Holy Family Association were chosen to stand vigil with Kateri. With the permission of Fr. Cholenec, one of the young women, Marguerite, was allowed to go and scourge herself to obtain a "happy death" for Kateri. Kateri beckoned to her upon her return and whispered encouragement to her that Marguerite was on the road to heaven. Marguerite saw herself as a wretched sinner, but Kateri begged Marguerite to pray for her after her death so she could go through purgatory and then be able repay Marguerite for her prayers with heavenly favors.[6]

Kateri spent the hours of the night communing with Jesus and Mary in prayer, but in the morning, her breathing became so shallow that Mary Theresa wondered if each breath would be her last. The Triduum of Holy Thursday, Good Friday, and Easter were fast approaching, so enough firewood would need to be gathered beforehand. Mary Theresa did not want to leave Kateri, but Fr. Cholenec encouraged her and the others to go, telling them they would be summoned if her death was imminent.

Only an hour after the women had ventured out, Kateri faintly called for Mary Theresa, who arrived as Fr. Cholenec was giving Kateri the last rites. Kateri managed, in her failing voice, to tell her weeping friend to keep strong in her faith or Kateri would accuse her before God. She exhorted Mary Theresa to continue with penance and to resist getting married. The special bond between Kateri and Mary Theresa strengthened all the more as Kateri commissioned her dearest companion to persevere in the same way that they had done together, knowing that they each would continue to pray for each other.

Fr. Cholenec began the last rites, which included confession, the anointing of the sick, and Holy Communion (called in Latin "Viaticum," meaning "provision for a journey"). This beautiful young woman was prepared for her next big step, entering into the loving arms of her eternal spouse, Jesus.

At three o'clock, the bells of St. Francis Xavier rang out to alert everyone that Kateri was ready to leave them. Mary Theresa returned to Kateri's side, holding her hand and caressing her cheek with her fingers. Fr. Cholenec and Fr. Chaucheteire offered prayers and words of encouragement until the final moment came when Kateri lifted her eyes to heaven and softly said, "Jesus, Mary."[7] The other women hurried into the house at the time Kateri reached the throes of death.

Her breathing was labored, and she spoke no more as Fr. Cholenec released her soul to Jesus with the prayer for the dying.

At 4:00 P.M., April 17, 1680, Kateri slipped into what seemed like a deep sleep, but Fr. Cholenec looked closer and discovered that she had died.[8] Fr. Cholenec remarked in his biography of her that Kateri celebrated in heaven two of the most important days, Holy Thursday, with the institution of the Eucharist, and Good Friday, with the Veneration of the Cross. These two things, the Eucharist and the cross were so dear to her heart.[9] He believed she went directly to heaven, with no need for purgatory, a thought that Kateri would have opposed, thinking she was not the model of piety that everyone else saw.

Both priests reported that the features of Kateri's sickly and pockmarked face changed shortly after her death, becoming more beautiful than when she had been alive. Though neither Fr. Chauchetiere nor Fr. Cholenec's accounts say that Kateri's pockmarks *completely* disappeared, this is the tradition that has come to be believed. It is clear, however, that the serenity and beauty of her face impressed all those who came to look at her, and Fr. Cholenec believed that "a small ray of glory" from heaven was shining from her.[10]

The Natives came and kissed her hands and took away mementos of her, which Fr. Cholenec encouraged them to use as relics to aid in prayer and to ask for her intercession. All evening they came to admire her peaceful and beautiful countenance. Fr. Chauchetiere was amazed as he observed how the Natives were all witnesses to the great faith of Kateri. He became so intrigued with Kateri that he wanted to have her remains kept in the chapel, believing her body should be close to Christ as was her soul.[11] Yet Fr. Cholenec decided she should be buried in the cemetery, choosing the very spot she had pointed out to her companions a few months previous.

During night prayers on Wednesday and even on Good Friday, Fr. Cholenec revealed to those in attendance the great model of faith that Kateri had been. Many had not known well the quiet and demure young lady, but their grief was joined to the others in so many sobs that Fr. Cholenec could barely go on. Even those who had been suspect of her chastity were put to shame, and the woman who had once accused her spent many years regretting her misjudgment of Kateri. The effect of her death upon the others was remarkable. Much like the disciples who first realized that the Lord had risen, the people at Kanawake realized that a true treasure had been among them. A continued zeal for penance prevailed with those at Kanawake—especially with the women who strove to live life as single people so they could be completely devoted to Christ.

A Frenchman visiting the mission during that time built a wooden coffin for her, a custom not used for Native Americans, who traditionally buried their dead in shallow graves in a sitting position or laid them to rest on a platform in the forest. He had gazed upon her serene face and felt moved to do this act of kindness for her. The lid of the coffin was left off so all who wished could look upon her until she was lowered into the grave at three o'clock in the afternoon on Maundy Thursday.[12] One source mentions the paradox of how her face, which she had hidden most of her life, was now a radiant beacon for everyone to look upon.[13] Fr. Chaucheiere spent many hours in prayer, standing at her grave site.

A Time of Grace

The next experience to touch the mission was the appearance of Kateri to several people in visions. The first was to Fr. Chauchetiere only six days after Kateri's death. Early Easter Monday in his room, for two hours, Fr. Chauchetiere saw Kateri shining bright like the sun with her eyes raised to heaven. Though she did not speak to him, he saw images of things that later came to pass: a church toppling over and a Native being burned at the stake.[14]

Anastasia also had the blessing of seeing Kateri two days later. She was awakened from a deep sleep by the voice of Kateri calling her to get up and look at her. Kateri's appearance was once again surrounded by bright light. She held out to Anastasia the cross that was around her neck and said she loved the cross as much now as she had on earth. She wanted everyone at the mission to love the cross as she did. As she vanished, Anastasia was greatly consoled because she loved her and missed her so greatly. This appearance buoyed Anastasia for years to come.[15]

Mary Theresa also reported that Kateri came to her early one morning, knocking on the wall and calling for her. Kateri told her that she had come to say good-bye because she was on her way to heaven now and that Mary Theresa should tell the priest. Mary Theresa ran outside but could see nothing, though she could hear her voice, once again saying good-bye. She had another encounter on a day she had argued with her sister. Kateri appeared wrapped in her customary blue blanket and told Mary Theresa many things, including a reminder to keep her resolution not to be angry.

The last recorded vision was again to Fr. Chauchetiere more than a year after her death. Like an intense brilliant light, she appeared and instructed him to paint her portrait. He brushed up on his painting skills and painted a small portrait of her followed by several more, which he distributed for people to pray for miracles, cures, and favors through her intercession.

Those at the mission became more and more convinced about the sanctity of Kateri and were passionate to let others know about her. Fr.

Cholenec wrote her official hagiography, *Vie de Catherine Tegakouita,* which was published and distributed in 1696. His work stressed the purity of St. Kateri, evidenced by her vow of perpetual virginity. At the time of his writing, virginity was held in great esteem, in contrast to the cultural sexual practices of the Native Americans. A "pure savage" was truly a marvel among European readers. Fr. Cholenec also wrote letters to authorities in Europe extolling her virtues.[16] Fr. Chaucheteire penned her account, though it remained unpublished until 1887.

The list of people who were healed through her intercession was remarkable from the start. Among the healings were women surviving difficult childbirths, intestinal blockage, respiratory ailments, pain from rheumatism, small pox, and incurable sicknesses. Two years after her death, Fr. Cholenec commented that there were so many miraculous cures that the Jesuit missionaries at Kanawake stopped recording them, though they continued to occur continually and consistently.[17] Her humble grave site became a place of pilgrimage to those from the nearby French settlements.

During this period of time, the use of relics was prominent, so the practice of mixing holy remains with medicine was fairly common. Some ashes from her clothing and dust from her grave were mixed with medicinal powders and ointments to be administered to the sick. In 1684, the bones of Kateri were moved into the new chapel of St. Francis Xavier, where they were venerated as relics. Eventually, her skull and some of her bones were taken to the Mission at St. Regis, Akwesasne, another mission to the Native Americans, so she could be venerated there also, but in the 1760s there was a fire that destroyed the chapel and consumed Kateri's remains. Currently there are relics of her bones in several locations, including the Vatican. In 1972 her remains were placed in a marble tomb in the Church of St. Francis

Xavier, where they currently rest. On display as a relic is a portion of her left rib.

There was something undeniable happening at Kanawake due to the holy life and death of Kateri Tekakwitha. Because the idea of severe penance is shocking to us today, it may be hard to look at St. Kateri as an example to follow, especially for young women who often struggle with disorders such as anorexia or cutting, which are unhealthy forms of self-mortification. The difference between penance and self-mutilation comes down to intent. The one performing penance does it in order to achieve a level of holiness and unity with Christ, whereas a self-mutilator acts out of self-loathing and as a form of control over themselves. The line is very fine, however, since many of the Native Americans at Kanawake felt that, because they had been such terrible sinners, harsh punishment was necessary.

The exemplary virtue that we see in Kateri is her obedience to the Church and her total devotion to Christ. She put every ounce of energy she had into her faith and into what was a popular teaching at the time. In our day, penance is still a part of our faith, but the attitude toward it has shifted, partly because the attitude toward the body has shifted. The Church acknowledges in no uncertain terms that we are responsible to treat our bodies well because we are made in the image of God, as the *Catechism* explains in paragraph 364:

> Man, though made of body and soul, is a unity. Through his very bodily condition he sums up in himself the elements of the material world. Through him they are thus brought to their highest perfection and can raise their voice in praise freely given to the Creator. For this reason man may not despise his bodily life. Rather he is obliged to regard his body as good and to hold it in honor since God has created it and will raise it up on the last day.

Today the Church encourages us to use our energy to help others as a way to engage in self-denial and devotion. By reaching out to others, we are engaging in a different form of self-denial, and the benefits may be greater in the economy of God due to the overwhelming needs of the world. For example, many Native American people on reservations live in great poverty. There are many Catholic organizations already involved in their care that greatly benefit from charitable giving.

It should not seem far-fetched for us to imagine that Christianity followed a path of penance and self-mortification. To set itself apart from the indulgences of the world, the Church made a strong division from it, seeing the uselessness and folly. Our small penances pale in comparison to the death and torture of Christ, yet they show that we love him and appreciate what he has accomplished for us. Every small step of self-denial and penance is a step closer to uniting ourselves with Christ's suffering in which we can participate in the saving of souls. The idea of reparation for the sins of the world comes into play here, as we understand that there is a role for the body of Christ in the redemption of world.

Our North American culture has long abandoned severe ideas of self-denial, especially in the physical submission of the body. However, the Church has given us these injunctions of self-denial—fasting, almsgiving, and penance, usually prescribed in the form of prayer, in addition to putting others' needs before our own. Not everyone can join a convent or spend all their waking hours in prayer, penance, and contemplation, but everyone can deny themselves, take up their cross, and follow the Lord.

Chapter Seven

332 YEARS TO SAINTHOOD

St. Kateri would have been the very last person to ever dream she was worthy of sainthood, but the Jesuits involved in her life, the Natives at Kanawake, and the settlers of the area couldn't help but be affected by her. Her grave became a place of pilgrimage, her name a prayer, and her love for Christ an inspiration. Portraits of her were hung in cabins. Dust from her grave was distributed to the sick. Letters and stories of her spread around the world as many people turned to this humble woman for help. Her story reached remote parts of the globe, but for many years the story seemed to fall on deaf ears in Rome.

In 1880, two hundred years after her death, a stirring of attention began in her homeland of the Mohawk Valley. By then, there were no Mohawks navigating the river in fur-laden canoes or tracking moose in the forest. No pulsing drums and melodious chants speaking to the spirits in the trees. No dreams or festivals. Gone was any evidence of Ossernenon and Caughnawaga. Instead farmers occupied these lands, and new industries had been built along the river. Here and there an arrowhead, bead necklace, axe, or pottery shard turned up with the farmer's plow, and collectors spirited the finds away.

At the time of St. Kateri's death, the territory under the control of the Iroquois League was at its greatest, stretching from the north shore of

Chesapeake Bay down through Kentucky to where the Mississippi and Ohio Rivers converge, as well as in the areas around Lake Michigan, southern Ontario, southwestern Quebec, northern New England, New York, and Pennsylvania. By the time of the American Revolution, however, their presence and influence had retreated back to their homeland in New York—and then a major blow ended Iroquois power.

Because the Iroquois had sided with the British against the American colonists in the War of Independence, they found themselves with no European ally after Britain's defeat. The Americans invaded the Iroquois homeland in 1779, driving the Iroquois population across the St. Lawrence into Canada, where a large amount of Iroquois still live today. Iroquois land was given to speculators through treaties, and in the early 1800s the U.S. government relocated most of the Iroquois who had not gone to Canada to reservations as far away as Oklahoma. Many Mohawks now live at Akwasasne, the Six Nations Reserve, and Kanawake, where St. Kateri spent the last four years of her life.

A Story That Must Be Told

In a land once dominated by the fierce Mohawk tribe, a young woman residing in New York named Ellen Walworth became intrigued by the dramatic stories of the Mohawk maiden. Her uncle, Fr. Clarence Walworth, became the rector of St. Mary's Church in Albany, and he learned of the story of the Jesuit martyrs and the missions they had started in Iroquois country not far down the road from Albany. When he told his curious niece about it, suggesting that she write a book about "The Lily of the Mohawk," as St. Kateri was already termed, the idea captivated Ellen, and she dove into the project with gusto.

She wrote, "The thought of a mere Indian girl reared in the forest among barbarians, yet winning for herself such titles as 'The Lily of the Mohawks' and 'The Genevieve of New France' recurred to my mind again and again, until it led me to a fixed determination to explore so tempting a field of romance and archaeology."[1]

She visited Montreal and Kanawake to pore over the Jesuit records, meticulously taking notes. She became acquainted with General John S. Clark, who not only supplied her with locations of the old sites of the Mohawk villages, but also guided her and her uncle on a week's tour of the Mohawk Valley. She even went to Paris in search of Fr. Felix Martin, S.J., who was editor of *The Jesuit Relations* and author of *Une Vierge Iroquoise*. Ellen's determination to present the life of the Iroquois virgin to the world culminated in the amazing story *The Life and Times of Kateri Tekakwitha: The Lily of the Mohawks*, published in 1891. It was the first English book of magnitude on Kateri's life. Shortly before her book came out, Fr. Claude Chauchetiere's overlooked biography of St. Kateri was finally published in 1887, as well.

Fr. Walworth was as captivated by Kateri as his niece, and he had a monument placed over Kateri's gravesite in Canada, where it remains to this day on a simple spot on the side of a roadway, occasionally visited by pilgrims. Across the top of the marker he had inscribed:

Kateri Tekakwitha
Ownkeonweke Katsitsiio Teonsitsianekaron.

Translated from the Iroquois, it means, "The fairest flower that ever bloomed among Native Americans."

Momentum toward Kateri's sainthood continued steadily, as cardinals and bishops from the United States and Canada, as well as Native American tribes, persisted in their requests for her cause to be reviewed, with a major push occurring in the 1930s. Finally, in 1939 an investigation of Kateri's cause began in earnest by the Congregation for the Causes of Saints. They reviewed the gathered documents, mostly from

The Jesuit Relations and Fr. Cholenec's account, as well as the testimonies of those who were healed after praying to her or coming in contact with a relic. Her life was deemed one of heroic Christian virtue, and Pope Pius XII declared her Venerable on January 3, 1943. This was cause for great celebration among the Native American Catholics who had prayed so fervently this prayer for her beatification:

> O God, who among the manifold marvels of Thy Grace in the New World, didst cause to blossom on the banks of the Mohawk and of the St. Lawrence, the pure and tender Lily, Catherine Tekakwitha, grant, we beseech Thee, the favor we beg through her intercession _____ that this Little Lover of Jesus and of His Cross may soon be raised to the honors of the altar by Holy Mother Church, and that our hearts may be enkindled with a stronger desire to imitate her innocence and faith. Through the same Christ Our Lord. Amen.[2]

CHAMPIONS OF THE CAUSE

One of the most instrumental Jesuits of the twentieth century to bring to light the virtue of St. Kateri was Fr. Henri Bechard, a man known for his optimism and continual smile. In 1948, he became the Jesuit in charge of the St. Francis Xavier Mission at Kanawake. One year later he was made vice-postulator for the cause of Kateri Tekakwitha, and he spent the next forty-two years of his life trying to encourage devotion to her. He began a quarterly publication, *Kateri Magazine*, which pleaded for prayers, donations, testimonials, and pledges, all in the ongoing attempt to move Kateri from venerable toward beatification. The magazine expressed regret that, while other venerables were deemed blessed, Kateri seemed to be continually overlooked, even as thousands attested to her intercession and groups all around the world from Germany to Samoa found inspiration from this humble woman.

Those who received favors wrote in with testimonials and donations. One such testimony was from a woman who said that her child, who suffered greatly from epileptic seizures, was cured by wearing a medal with an image of Kateri. Others were protected while traveling, gained employment, healed of a multitude of pains and ailments, and granted many unnamed favors. A continual stream of healings and miracles flowed from the intercession of Kateri from the days immediately after her death to some three hundred years later.

Another person to make a major impact in the revelation of St. Kateri was Fr. Thomas Grassman, a Conventual Franciscan, who in 1950 began to explore the Mohawk village site on the property in Fonda, New York, after it had been designated in 1938 as grounds for a future shrine. He dug around and found post molds from the stockade surrounding the village. Fr. Grassman and many volunteers excavated the Mohawk village, finding the layout of twelve longhouses and many artifacts that they housed in a museum on the grounds.

They renovated an old barn, creating a museum on the lower floor and a church on the main floor, which they named St. Peter's after the chapel from Kateri's days at Caughnawaga. This site was believed to be the Caughnawaga village location where Kateri was baptized in 1676.[3] The site developed over time and became a touch point between pilgrims of the twentieth century and the Mohawk maiden from the seventeenth century, a place where they could walk the same woods and drink from the same spring as Kateri. Mohawks from Akwasasne frequented the shrine, feeling the connection to her and also to their native land.

Several decades rolled by, as Native American Christians from many different tribes fervently prayed for her canonization. Fr. Bechard did all he could to rally people, and a group that had formed in 1939 called the Tekakwitha Conference urged those involved to pray, resulting in the formation of small groups called Kateri Circles on reservations and in churches. Then the long-awaited day arrived, when Pope John Paul II, who beatified more saints than any other pope in history, declared her Blessed on June 22, 1980. Fr. Bechard could hardly contain his joy, as he attended the beatification along with many Native Americans from Kanawake and across North America. Four other people who had labored for the salvation of Native Americans were beatified the same day.

That day, as Fr. Bechard gazed out the window overlooking St. Peter's Basilica, perhaps he felt not only Kateri near him, but the presence of his brother priests who were actual witnesses to Kateri's life and were compelled to let others know about her: Fr. Cholenec, Fr. Chauchetiere, Fr. De Lamberville, Fr. Fremin, Fr. Martin. The presence of the North American Martyrs who died at Ossernenon must have been felt by Fr. Bechard also: St. Isaac Jogues, St. Rene Goupil, St. John Lelande. The day commemorated the cumulative fruit of the labors of this string of Jesuits. Fr. Bechard penned these words on the eve of Kateri's beatification: "Since Blessed Kateri Tekakwitha, in the face of illness, hardships, and a whole motley of suffering, did correspond so generously each day to God's saving grace, should we not be ready to admire her, to imitate her, and ask her as a close friend to intercede for all of us?"[4]

The process of beatification requires verifying two miracles, one of which must occur after a person is named "Blessed." In the case of St. Kateri, all of the many attested miracles over three centuries were combined to account for her first miracle. During the beatification ceremony, Pope John Paul II summarized her life thus:

She spent her short life partly in what is now the state of New York and partly in Canada. She is a kind, gentle, and hardworking person, spending her time working, praying, and meditating. At the age of twenty she receives Baptism. Even when following her tribe in the hunting seasons, she continues her devotions, before a rough cross carved by herself in the forest. When her family urges her to marry, she replies very serenely and calmly that she has Jesus as her only spouse. This decision, in view of the social conditions of women in the Indian Tribes at the time, exposes Kateri to the risk of living as outcast and in poverty. It is a bold, unusual, and prophetic gesture: on 25 March, 1679, at the age of twenty-three, with the consent of her spiritual director, Kateri takes a vow of perpetual virginity—as far as we know, the first time that this was done among the North American Indians.

The last months of her life are an ever clearer manifestation of her solid faith, straight-forward humility, calm resignation, and radiant joy, even in the midst of terrible sufferings. Her last words, simple and sublime, whispered at the moment of her death, sum up, like a noble hymn, a life of purest charity: "Jesus, I love you..."[5]

As soon as Kateri was declared Blessed, faithful devotees began calling upon her in order to gain the needed miracle to advance her to sainthood. Another sixteen years passed until this occurred. In the meantime, Fr. Bechard died in 1990, never seeing Kateri canonized, though surely he was with her in heaven on that longed-for day. He left a wealth of information about her as a legacy, including his book printed in French, *Kaia'tano:ron Kateri Tekakwitha*.

ONE MORE MIRACLE

In 2006, a six-year-old boy named Jake Finkbonner of Ferndale, Washington, of Lummi descent, was happily playing a game of basketball. As he tossed the ball up into the net, another boy from the opposing team collided with Jake and propelled him into the basketball stand where he hit his lip, causing a small puncture. His mother Elsa took care of the abrasion, and they went on their way. As the day wore on, however, Jake's lip began to swell, and by two in the morning he was crying in great pain. After a trip to the emergency room at Seattle Children's Hospital, they waited to find out why this small cut was causing such pain and swelling.

Elsa and Don were not prepared to hear the doctor's words. "Your son had necrotizing fasciitis, or flesh-eating disease. The bacteria entered his lip and went into his blood stream when he his mouth hit the ball stand. This is an aggressive disease, and we will need to start treatment immediately. He will have to be intubated now because the swelling will cut off his airways. The affected areas will need surgery."

One of Elsa's first thoughts was to call their parish priest, Fr. Tim Sauer, who had baptized Jake. When he heard of the severity of the disease, he dropped everything and rushed to the hospital. He contacted members of the parish to begin praying to Blessed Kateri for a miracle, and soon a network of Kateri Circles joined in.

Jake underwent daily surgeries, as the doctors tried to stop the spread of the disease from lip to cheek to eyelids, scalp, and chest. They pumped fifteen different drugs into his little system and kept him in a hyperbaric chamber after each surgery. Each day the news was bleak, but the doctors kept trying.

A friend of the family brought a medal of Blessed Kateri to encourage them that many were praying fervently for a miracle. Then came a visit from Sr. Kateri Mitchell, the executive director of the Tekakwitha Conference and a Mohawk member of the Sisters of St. Anne from the St. Regis Mission at Akwasasne. She came with a precious relic of

Blessed Kateri, a piece of her wrist bone. As she entered the hospital room where his distraught parents sat near their bandaged young son, she took the relic and placed it upon Jake and prayed spontaneous prayers to Blessed Kateri for a miraculous healing. Sr. Kateri, who had taken the religious name of Kateri upon her vows in 1959, was a channel of amazing grace on that day. The common practice of recycling family names among the Iroquois was spiritually endowed at this moment, as the spirit of Blessed Kateri joined with her earthly kinswoman.

The doctors planned to attempt one last surgery to try and save Jake's life. His parents and family waited for the news in the same consultation room that had brought nothing but unhappy memories thus far. Then one of the doctors said these amazing words: "I think it has stopped."

In a surge of hope and gratitude, the family watched as Jake recovered from the disease, even though it did leave scars behind. He, like Blessed Kateri, had survived a deadly disease as a young child and came through with the marks remaining upon his flesh. As Jake grew older, he realized the connection he had to this wonder worker, Blessed Kateri.

News of Jake's recovery spread like wildfire, and those who had been praying felt this surely must be the miracle needed to elevate Blessed Kateri to sainthood. After careful review of the case, on December 19, 2011, the Church declared that indeed this healing was a miracle. The official day for Kateri's canonization would be October 21, 2012.

Six years after Sr. Kateri had prayed in the Seattle hospital room, she again saw Jake Finkbonner, but this time they were both standing in Rome for the canonization of Blessed Kateri Tekakwitha. Now, as they embraced, Jake was a young man of twelve. This moment was not only the culmination of the miraculous moment in the hospital room, but also a bonding to one another for being the instruments that propelled Blessed Kateri to the last step to sainthood, something neither took lightly.

Braids, feathers, drums, and embroidered clothing identified groups of Native Americans amid the throng of excited spectators in St. Peter's Square, as they awaited the moment Pope Benedict XVI would enroll Kateri into the canon of saints. For these groups, the healing symbol of Kateri brings their culture and their faith together, and it was clear that the Church recognized the contribution of the Native Americans to the faith. Though the ceremony itself was a solemn one, jubilation was undeniable. Those who could not make the long journey watched via television and were joined in spirit to their kinspeople as the relics of St. Kateri were venerated and the pope declared her a saint. The event was celebrated with Masses at shrines and churches all across North America.

In 332 years, North America has changed dramatically, but the simplicity of St. Kateri has not. Her message of complete devotion to Jesus echoes through the centuries to declare to the modern world that nothing else matters except one's relationship with Christ.

Chapter Eight

ST. KATERI AND NATIVE AMERICANS TODAY

There have been contrasting perceptions of St. Kateri among Catholics. The non-Natives look at her conversion as a leap from the pagan world to Catholicism, whereas the Native American Christians view her conversion as a continuation of her Native American heritage, not a separation from it. Many accounts of St. Kateri's life emphasize that she rose above her Native American spirituality to become a Christian, but over the centuries, her Native American heritage has been shown to be a vital part of who she was. This book is intends to present St. Kateri as both a devout Catholic and a spiritual Native American.

Blessed John Paul II recognized the nature of St. Kateri in his address to the Meeting of Native Americans on his visit to the United States in 1987. He said:

> Even when she dedicated herself fully to Jesus Christ, to the point of taking the prophetic step of making a vow of perpetual virginity, *she always remained what she was, a true daughter of her people*, following her tribe in the hunting seasons and continuing her devotions in the environment most suited to her way of life, before a rough cross carved by herself in the forest. The Gospel of Jesus Christ, which is the great gift of God's love, is never in contrast with what is noble and pure in the life of any tribe or nation, since all good things are his gifts.[1]

John Paul II's clarification helped to bring a deeper understanding of St. Kateri's identity. That she is considered patroness of the environment is based totally upon her Native American upbringing. Being one of the first Native American saints (St. Juan Diego is the only other one from this time) puts her in the position unlike any saint from the Old World: She has ties to the earth in a way that non-Natives can admire yet never completely grasp. She was part of a culture in which everything that was hunted or harvested for food, clothing, or shelter was received with a prayer of thanks for the offering that the animal or plant was making.

Exploitation of the earth's resources was foreign to Native Americans like Kateri. Once fresh and pristine, the lakes and rivers of North America are now polluted with industrial waste, chemical runoff, and toxic materials. Yet the deep respect for the earth and an understanding of the sacredness of creation is innate within the spirituality of the Iroquois. One hopes St. Kateri can help North America to discover how to use only the natural resources it needs and to be grateful for those it has. At her canonization, two images on bronze medallions placed in a glass box alongside a relic of her depict her deep in prayer on her knees in the woods. The image of the natural setting of the forest was a connection between her faith and her environment.

A NEED FOR HEALING

The sainthood of St. Kateri is also problematic for non-Christian Native Americans who believe that she had been manipulated by the Jesuits. The divide is as wide today between Christian and traditional Mohawks in the area of religion as it was in the seventeenth century, because it is hard for traditional Mohawks to understand why a Native American would leave the beauty of her own spirituality for something else unless he or she were forced or deceived.

St. Kateri is a thorn to those who believe that the Jesuits dominated her and used her as a pawn. Because of this frustration, some have even threatened to burn down her shrine in Fonda.[2] The hostility toward conversion still smolders, but this is not directed toward fellow Native Americans, because they are kin. Their anger is with the Church, which they believe has made St. Kateri into something she is not. The truth is, though, that St. Kateri chose to follow Christ of her own free will, as did hundreds of other Native Americans. Conversion filled a longing in their hearts for a deep relationship with Christ—on a level they could never completely experience in the spirituality of their native religion.

An exploration of the life of St. Kateri and her impact upon North America makes it impossible to be unaware of the many hurts felt by her Native American people today. The past mistreatment by the governments of the U.S. and Canada has had a huge impact on Native Americans, who lost their struggle to remain on their traditional homelands. They were removed from the ancestral tribal lands they considered sacred and were displaced onto reservations hundreds of miles away that could not sustain their traditional style of living. Cruel attempts to make the Native Americans like the rest of the North American population through forced boarding schools and denial of their Native ways are an embarrassment to a civilized world. It is ironic that at the same time the United States was fighting for the abolition of slavery, the U.S. Army was rounding up and killing Native Americans, banishing them to reservations, stripping them of their freedom, and leaving them in extreme poverty. The painful reality needs to be acknowledged as unjust.

Pope John Paul II recognized the need to apologize to the Native Americans for their marginalization and mistreatment. In his Apostolic Exhortation to America, he offered comments on a number of related topics:

Discrimination against indigenous peoples and Americans of African descent

If the Church in America, in fidelity to the Gospel of Christ, intends to walk the path of solidarity, she must devote special attention to those ethnic groups that even today experience discrimination. Every attempt to marginalize the indigenous peoples must be eliminated. This means, first of all, respecting their territories and the pacts made with them; likewise, efforts must be made to satisfy their legitimate social, health and cultural requirements. And how can we overlook the need for reconciliation between the indigenous peoples and the societies in which they are living?[3]

Preferential love for the poor and the outcast

"The Church in America must incarnate in her pastoral initiatives the solidarity of the universal Church towards the poor and the outcast of every kind. Her attitude needs to be one of assistance, promotion, liberation, and fraternal openness. The goal of the Church is to ensure that no one is marginalized." The memory of the dark chapters of America's history, involving the practice of slavery and other situations of social discrimination, must awaken a sincere desire for conversion leading to reconciliation and communion.[4]

This issue of discrimination is one that the Church is attempting to address. In 1991, a statement of the National Conference of Catholic Bishops on Native Americans encouraged "all Americans to better understand the role of native peoples in our history and to respond to the just grievances of our Native American brothers and sisters. We hope that this will be a graced time for rejecting all forms of racism."[5]

Through the recognition of St. Kateri Tekakwitha as a saint, an awareness of her people and all Native Americans will bring to the forefront issues that have long been ignored. Through her intercession, we can pray for justice for the indigenous people of North America, as well as for their continued conversion. Some Americans are hardly aware of Native Americans unless they live near a reservation, for, due to concerns about cultural sensitivity, many images of Native Americans have vanished from advertising, sports, cartoons, toys, and the media. They have disappeared from view. Very few adults know about forced boarding schools or the encroachment on tribal lands, which are still occurring to this day. St. Kateri will help North America to see the truth.

The nation of Canada has made apologies to the Native Americans in 1998 and 2008 for forcing their children to attend schools that removed them from their native way of life and for forbidding them from speaking their native language or practicing anything of their traditions.[6] The U.S. has not publicly apologized for the same behavior, but we can pray that this will happen. Pope Benedict the XVI on his first visit to the U.S. in April 2008 made reference in his homily to the injustices against the Native Americans and African Americans, pointing out that not all Americans have been given the promise of hope.[7]

Wounds within the Native American soul need healing, but the intercession of St. Kateri can help make this happen. She always encouraged others to live for Jesus in purity and holiness, and her influence is felt among those who have prayed for her canonization for many years. The Church should engage in praying for reparation for any injustice done to Native Americans and all ethnic groups who have been unjustly treated.

The words of the Divine Mercy Chaplet are very appropriate for this situation. "Eternal Father, I offer you the Body and Blood, Soul and Divinity, of Your Dearly Beloved Son, Our Lord, Jesus Christ, in atonement for our sins and those of the whole world. For the sake of His sorrowful Passion, have mercy on us and on the whole world."

This prayer is one that St. Kateri would definitely have prayed with great sincerity had it been written in her time. Through extreme acts of penance, she gave her own body, united with Christ in atonement for the sins of herself and her people. She would have identified with the prayer by adding her own sacrifice for God's mercy on the world.

THE CHURCH'S VITAL ROLE

The Catholic Church can also play a vital role in assisting those in need on many reservations throughout the United States and Canada. There are many Catholic organizations serving the poor and needy on reservations, and Christians can support them through prayers, donations, and service projects. There are organizations within the Native American Christian community that are trying to rebuild the Catholic traditions among the baptized and to strengthen their ties to the Church. The Tekakwitha Conference has evolved into an organization that brings together Native American Catholics, priests, religious, and laypeople to dialogue on issues relevant to Native Americans. Currently, the conference is overseen by Archbishop Charles Chaput, who is himself one-quarter Native American, from the Potawatomi Tribe.

The Conference of U.S. Bishops Ad Hoc committee made an attempt in 1999 to get a pulse on the state of Native American Catholics, with the intent of better meeting their needs. They found that in 2000, 4.1 million people claimed to be of some Native American ancestry, with 40 percent living on reservations or trust lands.[8] Approximately 21 percent of those who indicated Native American ancestry also called themselves Catholic. Over the past 300 years, 158 Native American tribes have been served by hundreds of missionaries in the U.S.[9]

With the findings of the committee, an effort is being made to pinpoint ways in which more Native Americans can be encouraged to enter religious life in order to serve their communities and for dioceses to establish plans to better serve Native Americans if there are groups within their area. A better awareness of Native Americans for all Catholics will help the Church in her mission to strengthen Catholic practice and growth.

The enculturation of Native American rituals and symbols into the liturgy is also an ongoing issue to be determined with dialogue and understanding. There are many practices used by Native American Catholics in liturgies such as smudging, a ceremonial burning of herbs, drums and dancing, and native designs on vessels and vestments. There are many traditions and symbols that mean something to one tribal group but not another.

While the practices may be diverse, St. Kateri Tekakwitha is an enduring feature in sculpture, paintings, stained glass, and on prayer cards among all Native American Catholics. Undoubtedly, she is a unifying factor among the Native Americans—and can also be a unifying factor to bring together Natives and non-Natives under her patronage. Humble, holy St. Kateri intercedes for her people, for the Church, for North America. St. Kateri Tekakwitha, pray for us!

Chapter Nine

A PILGRIM'S GUIDE TO THE LAND OF ST. KATERI

A pilgrimage to the native lands of St. Kateri Tekakwitha converges on the Mohawk Valley in present day New York, which spreads from Albany on the east and follows the Mohawk River westward to Syracuse. Along that route is the **National Shrine of St. Kateri Tekakwitha** in Fonda, New York, which commemorates the town in which she lived at the time of her baptism. There is an archeological site of the town of Caughnawaga, a museum, a gift shop, a candle chapel, and a meditative walkway on the shrine grounds.

Only a short distance from this shrine is the **Shrine of the North American Martyrs**, located near the town of Auriesville. This interesting site commemorates the martyrdom of the three Jesuit missionaries St. Isaac Jogues, St. René Goupil, and St. John Lelande—who were martyred in 1642 and 1646 by the Mohawks about ten years before St. Kateri's birth.

This shrine has a large coliseum built with a rustic interior, a gift shop, museums, and a walk through a ravine that commemorates where the bodies of the martyrs were thrown. Both shrines afford ample opportunity for learning as well as spiritual meditation and reflection.

National Shrine of St. Kateri Tekakwitha—www.katerishrine.com

Shrine of the North American Martyrs—www.martyrshrine.com

Other places of interest in the vicinity of the shrines can be found within an hour's drive. The **New York State Museum** in Albany displays an authentically constructed Iroquois longhouse and many artifacts and dioramas of Iroquois life. Dinner at the historic **Glen Sanders Mansion** in New Scotia, New York, on the banks of the Mohawk River, is reminiscent of the era when the Iroquois dealt with the Dutch fur traders near this location. The **Iroquois Indian Museum** is located near Howes Cave, New York, and displays Iroquois art through the centuries. It is open during the summer and has several lovely nature walks nearby.

West of the National Shrine of St. Kateri Tekakwitha is a small community of Mohawks who have moved back into the valley and live in community there. They operate the **Kanantsiohareke Gift Shop**, which offers native crafts, books, and wampum.

New York State Museum—www.nysm.nysed.gov/

Glen Sanders Mansion—www.glensandersmansion.com/

Iroquois Indian Museum—www.iroquoismuseum.org/

Kanantsiohareke Mohawk Gift Shop—www.mohawkcommunity. com/

In Syracuse, New York, a visit to **St. Marie among the Iroquois Living History Museum**, which is a recreation of the Jesuit mission, hails back to the seventeenth century at the time of St. Kateri's birth. This mission was in operation from 1656–1658 in the heart of Iroquois territory in Onondaga. To the east of Syracuse is the small town of Herkimer, where the **Herkimer Diamond Mines** are located. Here there are mining opportunities, a gift shop, a geological museum, and a KOA campground. The Herkimer diamond was originally traded by the Iroquois.

St. Marie among the Iroquois Living History Museum— onondagacountyparks.com/sainte-marie-among-the-iroquois

The Herkimer Diamond Mines—www.herkimerdiamond.com/ Traveling north from Albany, one can follow St. Kateri's journey from her homeland to the mission at LaPrairie, Canada, in 1676. Her remains are now located in the **Church of St. Francis Xavier in Kanawake**, just outside the city of Montreal, Canada. Also on display in the church are many statues and religious items, some from the seventeenth century, including a silver monstrance that was in the church where St. Kateri attended daily Mass. The first known painting of St. Kateri by Fr. Claude Chauchetiere, circa 1685, is on display here.

Church of St. Francis Xavier in Kanawake—kateritekakwitha.net/ st-francis-xavier-mission/

Also in Montreal is the **St. Marguerite Bourgeoys Museum**, which displays the archaeological remains of a Native American campsite as well as the seventeenth-century settlement and chapel built for pilgrims by the pioneer woman, St. Marguerite Bourgeoys, over three hundred years ago.

St. Marguerite Bourgeoys Museum—www.marguerite-bourgeoys. com

In Ontario, Canada, the town of Midland is where the **Mission among the Hurons** was located. There is a living history museum with several different programs, from canoe travel on the St. Lawrence to experiencing seventeenth-century mission life with costumed actors. Nearby is the **Martyrs' Shrine**, which commemorates the eight North American Martyrs and also houses the remains of two martyrs, St. Jean de Brebeuf and St. Gabriel Lalemant.

Mission among the Hurons—www.saintemarieamongthehurons. on.ca

Martyrs' Shrine—www.martyrs-shrine.com/

Other locations throughout the U.S. and Canada include, but are by no means limited to:

St. Joseph Mission, Deer River, Minnesota

St. Charles Church, Cass Lake, Minnesota

National Basilica of the Immaculate Conception, Washington, D.C.

Shrine of Our Lady of Guadalupe, LaCrosse, Wisconsin

National Shrine Basilica of Our Lady of Fatima, Lewiston, New York

St. Lucy's Church, Syracuse, New York

St. Patrick's Cathedral, New York, New York

St. John's University, Collegeville, Minnesota

Sioux Mission of St. Francis, Rosebud, South Dakota

North American Martyrs' Shrine-Church, Peekskill, New York, grotto of St. Kateri

PRAYERS TO RECITE ON PILGRIMAGE

St. Kateri Indian Rosary

This is a rosary designed with a total of twenty-four beads, one for each year of Kateri's life. The beads are divided into three sections of eight: brown, red, and clear. Brown represents the earth, and the Our Father is recited on each of these; red is the color of blood, and the Hail Mary is recited on each of these; clear is the color of water, and the Glory Be is recited on each of these.

The Rosary

This prayer was taught to all the Native American converts as part of their daily practice.

Divine Mercy Prayer

This prayer is important to pray for the reparation of sins against the Native Americans.

Prayers of Intercession to St. Kateri Tekakwitha

Oh St. Kateri Tekakwitha, in your life you experienced pain, sorrow, and hardship. Yet in all things you found joy and peace in believing in Jesus, present to us in the Eucharist and in his love expressed to us on the cross.

O Great Lily of the Mohawks, we ask that you take our intentions (state your intention) to the foot of the cross. Ask Jesus, our loving Savior, to bring healing to those who are heavily burdened. Through your intercession, may this favor be granted if it is according to the will of God.

By your prayer, help us always to remain faithful to Jesus and to his Holy Church.

St. Kateri Tekakwitha, pray for us. Amen.

Loving Creator, we acknowledge your power and presence in the four directions of your vast and beautiful universe. We celebrate St. Kateri Tekakwitha, Lily of the Mohawks, as one of your Son's most faithful followers. Help us to turn our backs on all evil and walk in her footsteps, sharing love and Christian concern with others. Let us reverence, as she did, your mystical presence in the poor and suffering.

Through Kateri's powerful intercession, we confidently ask you to grant us this special favor (state intention) in her name. Share your healing and peace especially with my family, friends, and the sick, who we commend to your loving care. We ask this through your crucified and risen Son, Our Lord Jesus Christ, the eternal Word, who lives and reigns with you forever and ever. Amen.

St. Kateri, maiden so pure, Christian so faithful, lover so kind, we call on you with faith and hope, to intercede with our Lord Jesus to bring physical, emotional, and spiritual healing to our friend (mention name).

We believe that Jesus heals. We believe that Jesus wants good things for us. And so we make our prayer with the confidence and the fervent expectation that something wondrous, something powerful, something life-giving will happen.

St. Kateri, help us to be as pure and faithful and loving as you.

Inspire us to believe as you have believed in the presence and power of Our Lord. Amen.

St. Kateri, bright star of love and faith, be my guide and guardian always.

St. Kateri, follower of purity and prayer, be my advocate before God, especially in my present need.

We ask this through Jesus Christ, Our Lord. Amen.

St. Kateri, Lily of the Mohawks, pray for us!

Litany of St. Kateri

Lord, have mercy. *Lord, have mercy.*

Christ, have mercy. *Christ, have mercy.*

Lord, have mercy. *Lord, have mercy.*

Jesus, hear us. *Jesus, graciously hear us.*

God, the Father of Heaven, *have mercy on us.*

God the Son, Redeemer of the world, *have mercy on us.*

God, the Holy Spirit, *have mercy on us.*

Holy Trinity, One God, *have mercy on us.*

Holy St. Kateri Tekakwitha, *pray for us.*

Holy young virgin, *pray for us.*

Spouse of Christ, *pray for us.*

Daughter of Mary, Mother of God, *pray for us.*

Lily of purity, *pray for us.*

Consoler of the heart of Jesus, *pray for us.*

Lover of the cross of Jesus, *pray for us.*

Courage of the afflicted, *pray for us.*

Leader of the true faith through the love of Mary, Mother of God, *pray for us.*

Servant to the sick, *pray for us.*

Great servant of God, *pray for us.*

Spiritual sister, *pray for us.*

Guardian of chastity, *pray for us.*

Reliever of the temptations of the flesh, *pray for us.*

Imitator of our Lord in prayer, *pray for us.*

Deliverer of the persecuted, *pray for us.*

Virgin of patience, *pray for us.*

Virgin of penance, *pray for us.*

Virgin most obedient, *pray for us.*

Virgin most humble, *pray for us.*

Virgin, St. Kateri Tekakwitha, *pray for us.*

Lamb of God, who takes away the sins of the world, *spare us, O Lord!*

Lamb of God, who takes away the sins of the world, *graciously hear us, O Lord!*

Lamb of God, who takes away the sins of the world, *have mercy on us.*

Pray for us, O holy, daughter of the Mother of God, *that we find Christ through you, St. Kateri Tekakwitha.*

Let us pray. St. Kateri Tekakwitha, who made her mother the Immaculate Mary, Mother of God, and has given herself as the spouse to Christ, lead us on the road to heaven and without ever abandoning us during this travel, as God the Father had guided you in your voyage without ever abandoning you. Through you with your eternal spouse, Jesus Christ. *Amen.*

REFLECTIONS

Following are nine reflections for your pilgrimage, whether you visit the shrines in person or visit them in your heart. These reflections are based on the life of St. Kateri Tekakwitha and her spiritual journey.

1. Surrender

Surrender is a difficult word for us. Surrender equals defeat, failure, and unhappiness if we don't get our own way. We naturally feel we should have it all, should be on top, should do better. This struggle in our hearts between having our way and letting God have his way challenges us daily. Most often, we don't even realize there *is* a battle in our hearts to surrender our wills to Christ.

During St. Kateri's life, she lived—and thrived—through many difficult circumstances, including disease, the loss of her parents, famine, displacement, and persecution. The nature of her people was to accept what life and nature brought to them and to be prepared for the future. Food, shelter, and daily living were all attended to with no questions asked in a spirit of cooperation and working together for the common good of the community. Each person played a vital role. In such an environment, St. Kateri tended to the needs of others before her own because it was part of her upbringing and part of her gentle and kind nature. Her disposition led her to freely submit to Christ in all things, surrendering her own will in order to follow his.

May we imitate her virtue and give ourselves completely to Christ, trusting in his providence.

2. Silence

Silence has become an indicator that something is wrong. Why isn't the radio or television on? Why isn't my phone working? Why isn't anyone talking? Many of us feel uncomfortable with silence, but we need silence in order to hear the still, small voice of Christ calling us. We need time for our thoughts to focus on our interior and we can stop processing outside stimuli. Our minds and bodies need times of silence for self-reflection, prayer, and decision making.

St. Kateri lived in a time when silence was abundant. The solitude of the verdant forest created an atmosphere for prayer, which St. Kateri applied to her daily routine after her baptism. She would leave the business of the village to pray in the quiet forest, either in the chapel or before a wooden cross she carved into a tree. Especially silent were the days when a blanket of snow muffled the earth and even the birds and animals lingered longer in warm places.

Kneeling in the snow before the cross, St. Kateri could hear the voice of Christ calling her to a deeper relationship, which she followed with eagerness. She learned how to listen through her native people who were trained to be good listeners. In a conversation, a person spoke until he or she had said everything they had wanted to say, while the other person listened without interruption. Then the listener responded until he or she was finished, while the other person listened.

May we imitate her virtue of listening in prayer without interrupting the voice of God.

3. Learning

In our day and age, through the Internet, we have at our fingertips an endless opportunity for learning. We barely have to wonder anymore about anything since we can find the answer in mere seconds. Unknown to any previous generation is the staggering array of what we can access in an instant. Standard methods of learning that have been used for centuries are vanishing as schools and universities shift to new paradigms. The idea that better education can make mankind better is a dream that seems to be closer than ever.

When the Jesuits started their missions among the Native Americans, they were some of the most learned men in the world. They knew several languages, were trained in the arts, and were taught discipline along with all the standard academics of their day. Through their learning, they were able to translate the Gospel into Native American languages through the spoken word and illustrations of the Bible stories.

On the other hand, many Native Americans, like St. Kateri, were eager learners. They had incredible memory capacity, since all of their stories were learned by heart rather than written down. They memorized the lay of the land for hundreds of miles without the use of a map. Within the mind of a Native American elder was an amazing amount of knowledge. The sharp thinking of the Native Americans also helped them to adapt to new technologies in warfare introduced by the Europeans. St. Kateri learned the Gospel from the Jesuits at a remarkable rate, as is attested by her instructors who remarked that she learned in a few short months what took years for others to understand. Because of this, she was granted baptism after only a few months of instruction.

May we fill our minds with learning what is true and good.

4. Simplicity

The Iroquois way of life is based on simplicity. The implements needed for daily living were gathered from what was close at hand, from stone and bone to branch and berry. Their lives revolved around the organic things of the earth. In our world today, there is a trend toward the local and organic, but for the most part, what we eat and wear are manufactured from nonorganic sources from all parts of the world. We have so many choices that we can easily get caught up in the pursuit of things and busyness and lose sight of what is important. The Iroquois lifestyle found time to incorporate beauty and practicality, but balanced that with attending to the basics and to the cycle of life and its traditions. St. Kateri was content with her traditional way of life and contributed to beauty with her embroidery skills, all the while never neglecting her spiritual life.

May we be content with what we have and turn away from the temptation of always wanting more.

5. Prayer

Prayer is universal to humanity. The need to invoke the supernatural is part of every culture and society. Prayer can be a way to determine who we are. In understanding who created us, we obtain our identity. The Native Americans developed a systematic way of praying to the Creator, offering him thanks, and telling of the wonders of creation.

For the Iroquois, every feast began with a thanksgiving prayer to the Creator, so St. Kateri was well acquainted with the concept of prayer. When she realized what Christ had done for her in his suffering, she was very moved and spent much time in devotion to him in prayer. She rose very early every day to pray with her rosary, an integral part of the practice of Native American Christians. If anyone wondered where she was, the first place to look was at her prayer spot.

May we find fulfillment in who we are by spending time in communion with Christ through prayer.

6. Penance

Penance is a concept that is growing less and less prominent in modern society. We are more likely to blame someone else for a problem than to take responsibility for it ourselves. Without the discipline of frequent confession, we can drift away from the reality of our shortcomings. To be truly sorry for one's faults is undermined by the modern philosophy that everyone is "OK." If we are to achieve holiness, we must be honest about our faults and do penance for them.

St. Kateri was keenly aware of the sacrifice and suffering that Christ paid for her sins, and she was more than willing to recognize her part in Christ's suffering. Though she reached a mystical level in her forms of penance and few are called to such a walk with Christ, her life shows us a truly contrite heart. She did not fool herself with the notion that we want to entertain: "I am okay as I am."

May we mourn our sins and correct our lives with penance and contrition.

7. Reparation for the Sins of Our World

The brutality that humankind has shown to one another since Cain killed Abel has been evident in every generation. The Iroquois were masters of brutality toward their enemies, a fact that greatly grieved St. Kateri. Though she did not participate in the cruel tortures her tribe inflicted upon captives, she was deeply upset over this sin of her people. She understood that because people are a community, when one is guilty, all are guilty. Therefore, she wanted to make reparation for the sins of torture and cannibalism in order for God to show mercy. She also was deeply affected by Christ's sufferings and wanted to make reparation. Pope John Paul II defined reparation as the "unceasing effort to stand beside the endless crosses on which the Son of God continues to be crucified."[1]

Though the Divine Mercy Chaplet was not used yet in St. Kateri's time, it can be a wonderful method for us to make reparation for the sins of our own nations, for the brutality shown toward the unborn, for neglect of the poor, for sins against African Americans, and for the mistreatment of Native Americans.

Let us pray, "Lord, have mercy on us and on the whole world."

8. Sincerity

As Christians, one of our most needed characteristics is sincerity. In all that we say and do, we must consistently portray the goodness of Christ. We can usually spot a sincere person by their consistent behavior and reliable words. Just being around a genuine person gives us a boost.

St. Kateri was a woman with no guile who was filled with such an eagerness to please the Lord that it was contagious. Those who knew her attested that she was special in this way, and the fact that people flocked to her grave asking for healing right after her death speaks volumes about her example of Christ's charity. Many miracles occurred through her intercession, bringing to light that she was a true saint.

May our sincerity be a reflection of the nature of Christ for all the world to see.

9. Union with Christ

St. Kateri was able to keep her eyes focused on Christ throughout the difficulties that she faced. When she was accused of immorality, she focused on Christ as her spouse and did not lash out at her accuser. When those in her home village persecuted her for her love of Christ, she persisted in her devotion, undeterred by their taunts and tricks. When she was under pressure to marry, she desperately clung to the hope of remaining a virgin, to take Christ as her spouse. Shortly before her death she took a vow of virginity, something very rare among the Native Americans.

This dimension of her spirituality was countercultural to her Native American upbringing, in which women were expected to marry and premarital sex after puberty was common. To be a virgin was not considered a virtue among the Iroquois but St. Kateri's sole focus to be united forever with Christ was demonstrated in her earthly life with her vow of virginity. Nothing but pleasing Christ mattered to her.

May we be so in love with Christ that all else pales in comparison.

In 1980, the Mohawk Valley Project began with a systematic look through the region at over one hundred Mohawk villages. Countless hours of research and hard work went into locating these sites, categorizing the materials found, and bringing the information to publication. Dr. Dean Snow at Albany State University and William Starna of State University of New York College at Oneonta headed this project, and the fruit of their research can be found in *Mohawk Valley Archaeology: The Sites* and *Mohawk Valley Archaeology: The Collections*.

This research, one hundred years after the opening of the St. Kateri Shrine and the Shrine of the North American Martyrs, was not available at the time that Ellen Walworth, an early biographer of St. Kateri, searched for the towns of St. Kateri's life. The location of the current shrines, when identified in the 1880s, were as close an estimation to the actual locations as could be determined at the time and are today important places to visit. The site of the St. Kateri Shrine is, in fact, located near the archaeological site of Caughnawaga, but archaeological dating establishes that this site was built after St. Kateri had moved to the Sault mission near Montreal.

This new understanding in no way diminishes the spiritual significance of the St. Kateri Shrine, and we are to be thankful to Ellen Walworth and the Franciscans for their efforts to locate St. Kateri's past in order to make her life known and experienced by millions of Catholic pilgrims. The actual sites of the villages where St. Kateri lived are undisclosed, except to archaeological researchers, because they are on private property.

The shrines, by virtue of the devotion that pilgrims bring to them, are holy places. There, we can reflect on the beauty of the natural environment in which St. Kateri lived, see many artifacts from her time period, and most importantly, join with her in the holy sacrifice of the Mass.

BAUDER/OSSERNENON

Archaeological Site: Bauder Site

Site Number: 1122

Indigineous Name: Ossernenon

Current Name: None

Modern Location: Town of Root. East of Currytown Rd. on a spur of land overlooking Yatesville Creek.

North or South of Mohawk River: South

Dating: 1635–1646

Town Population: 725

Mohawk Population: 1,760

Came from/Moved to: From Cromwell Site to Printup Site/ Osserneon

European Political Power: Dutch

Jesuit Presence: St. Isaac Jogues held captive here 1642–1643. St. René Goupil martyred here and buried by St. Isaac Jogues in nearby ravine. St. Isaac Jogues & Jean Lelande martyred here in 1646.

Tie to Kateri: Kateri's father and uncle were alive at this site and perhaps ten to fifteen years old.

Identified by Walworth/Clark: none

Excavation Dates: No excavations. Surveyed by Rumrill and University at Albany. Generally known by end of the nineteenth century.

Current Condition: Unknown
Pages in Dean Snow, *Mohawk Valley Archaeology: The Sites,* 304–309
Significant Artifacts: gunflints, beads, iron axes, and knives

PRINTUP/OSSERNENON
Archaeological Site: Printup Site
Site Number: 1124
Indigenous Names: Osserrion, Asserue
Current Name: None
Modern Location: Town of Glen (Lusso Rd. and Van Epps). Jim
Francis, current owner on a bluff overlooking river, (farm was sold
around 2002 according to neighbor).
Dating: 1647–1659
North or South of Mohawk River: South
Town Population: 374
Mohawk Population: 1,734+570 Huron
Came from/Moved to: From Bauder site/Ossernenon to Freeman
site/Caughnawaga
European Political Power: Dutch. September 24, 1659, Dutch dele-
gation traveled there with trade goods to council meeting to renew
their friendship. Wanted assistance in building new site at Freeman
called Caughnawaga
Jesuit Presence: Jesuits visit between 1655 and 1658.
Tie to Kateri: Kateri Tekakwitha born here. Her father would have
been chief and interacted with the Dutch.
Identified by Walworth/Clark: Clark called it Andagoron; so did
Nelson Green. Andagoron was site visited by Isaac Jogues as a civilian
ambassador.
Excavation Dates: No formal excavations or survey. Generally known
by 1922.

Current Condition: Unknown/on private property

Pages in Dean Snow, *Mohawk Valley Archaeology: The Sites,* 365–371

Significant Artifacts: Many collections mislabel artifacts from here as from Andagoron. Incised Jesuit rings, Dutch pipes, gun parts, glass beads, cast lead shot and lead effigies, iron implements, dated coins.

Comments: A small stream one hundred meters south is the nearest source of running water.

FREEMAN/CAUGHNAWAGA

Archaeological Site: Freeman Site

Site Number: 1145

Indigenous Name: Caughnawaga

Current Name: None

Modern Location: Town of Root (Randall). Caughnawake Kaghnuwage. Andaraque. Intersection of Dillenbeck & Argersinger

Dating: 1659–1666

North or South of Mohawk River: South

Town Population: 374

Mohawk Population: 1,760

Came from/Moved to: From Printup site/Ossernenon to Fox Farm/ Caughnawaga

European Political Power: Dutch with threat of French

Jesuit Presence: No Jesuits. Site occupied during hiatus in their missionary activities that lasted from 1659–1667.

Tie to St. Kateri: Moved here after smallpox epidemic to live with her aunt and uncle. Town attacked by French, de Tracy. Village burned.

Identified by Walworth/Clark: None

Excavation Dates: No formal excavations or survey. Discovered after 1957, salvage excavations

Current Condition: Beneath home construction
Pages in Dean Snow, *Mohawk Valley Archaeology: The Sites,* 371–375
Significant Artifacts: Glass beads, iron gunlock, no Jesuit religious
artifacts, brass mouth harp, 1632 coin, native ceramics, brass arrow
heads.
Comments: Ash layer indicates it had been destroyed by fire. Rich
variety of soils and forest cover in immediate vicinity.

FOX FARM/CAUGHNAWAGA
Archaeological Site: Fox Farm Site
Site number: 1126
Indigenous Names: Caughnawaga, Cahaniaga, Kaghnuwage
Gandaougue, Kaghenewage
Current Name: None
Modern Location: Town of Mohawk. On a high bluff overlooking
the river
Dating: 1667–1679
North or South of Mohawk River: North
Town Population: 560
Mohawk Population: 2,000
Came from/Moved to: From Freeman site/Caughnawaga to Veeder
Site/Caughnawaga
European Political Power: French/Dutch battling. French win, then
Dutch win. Goes to British in 1674, renamed New York.
1677 Covenant Chain formed between Iroquois and English.
Jesuit Presence: Jesuits return—permanent missions at
Tionnontoguen, Caughnawaga, Onondaga until 1679.
1667 Fremin, Bruyas, Pierron spent three days in Kateri's lodge.
1674 Fr. Jacque de Lamberville comes.

Tie to Kateri: Kateri baptized here, Easter 1676. Moves away to Canada 1677.

Identified by Walworth/Clark: None

Excavation Dates: No formal survey. Unrecorded before it was used for gravel mine. Findings published in 1985.

Current Condition: Destroyed by gravel mining

Pages in Dean Snow, *Mohawk Valley Archaeology: The Sites,* 415–419

Significant Artifacts:

Comments: Site abandoned when Jesuits leave—Catholics to Canada, Mohawks to Veeder site.

1672 began migration of Catholic Mohawks to Canada. Same for Hurons living among the Mohawk.

VEEDER/CAUGHNAWAGA

Archaeological Site: Veeder Site

Site number: 1116

Indigenous Name: Caughnawaga

Current Name: Caughnawaga

Modern Location: Near Fonda, N.Y.

Dating: 1679–1693

North or South of Mohawk River: North

Town Population: 700

Mohawk Population: 2,000 based on Greenhalgh estimation

Came from/Moved to: From Fox Farm/Caughnawaga Mohawks moved south of river after destruction by French in 1693.

European Political Power: English in conflict with French

Jesuit Presence: Jesuit missions ended. They returned to New France in 1679.

Tie to Kateri: Kateri may have lived here very short while, but not here when town destroyed.

Identified by Walworth/Clark: Caughnawaga—considered it location where Kateri lived from 1667 until 1677. He did not know village relocated twice before, all bearing same name (Freeman, Fox Farm, Veeder).

Excavation Dates: General John S. Clark of Auburn included sketch from 1877 or the site. Fr. Grassman tested site in 1945. Excavations can be viewed today.

Current Condition: Shrine grounds of Kateri Tekakwitha owned by the Franciscans.

Pages in Dean Snow, *Mohawk Valley Archaeology: The Sites*, 431–436

Significant Artifacts: Many are on display at shrine's museum.

Comments: This is now a pilgrimage site.

Introduction

1. Other possible meanings of her name: One Who Places Things in Order; She Who Pushes with Her Hands; She Who Walks Groping for Her Way.

2. Claude Chauchetierc, S.J., *The Life of the Good Catherine Tekakwitha* (1695), chap. 9.

3. Darren Bonaparte, *A Lily Among Thorns: The Mohawk Repatriation of Kateri Tekakwitha* (The Mohawk Territory of Akwesasne: The Wampum Chronicles), p. 62.

4. Tom Porter, *Clanology: Clan System of the Iroquois* (Cornwall, Ontario: Native American Travelling College), p. 20.

5. Porter, *Clanology*, pp. 7–11.

6. Dean R. Snow, *Mohawk Valley Archaeology: The Collections* (University Park, Pennsylvania: Matson Museum of Anthropology, Pennsylvania State University, 1994), p. 60.

Chapter One

1. *Catechism of the Catholic Church* (Washington, D.C.. USCCB, 1997) 847–848.

2. Bechard, *Kateri Magazine* vol. 104, 24.

3. It is possible that Tekakwitha's mother's baptismal name was also Catherine, as research by Fr. Bechard shows there was an infant girl baptized on March 5, 1639, named Catherine. According to the "Catalogue of the deceased at the place named Trois-Rivieres" there are only four or five names of baptized baby girls that could be dated to Tekakwitha's mother (Bechard, KM vol. 104, p. 24).

4. See information about the Bauder Site in the Appendix.

5. *The Jesuit Relations*, vol. 31, p. 41.

6. *The Jesuit Relations*, vol. 31, pp. 53–57.

7. Reuben Gold Thwaites, *The Jesuit Relations and Allied Documents*, 1899.

8. Translation of The Great Law of Peace from Akwesasne Notes, 1977.

9. *The Jesuit Relations*, vol. 14, Chapter VI.

10. *The Jesuit Relations*, vol. 14, Chapter VI.

11. Chauchetiere, *The Life of the Good Catherine*, chap. 2.

12. *The Jesuit Relations*, vol. 22, Chapter XI.

13. See information about the Bauder Site in the Appendix.

14. Dean R. Snow, *Mohawk Valley Archaeology: The Sites*, 336.

Chapter Two

1. See information about the Printup Site in the Appendix.

2. *The Jesuit Relations*, vol. 42, Chapter I.

3. Freeman Site, Appendix.

4. This is based on the archaeological report that shows a drop in population from over 7,000 total Mohawks down to 2,000.

5. Arthur C. Aufderheide, Conrado Rodriguez-Martin, and Odin Langsjoen, *The Cambridge Encyclopedia of Human Paleopathology* (Cambridge: Cambridge University Press, 1998), p. 205.

6. One way in which we can surmise the age of Tekakwitha's mother is through the dates of the smallpox epidemics that swept through the Northwest Woodlands. The first epidemic hit among the Huron and northern tribes around 1634. Had she been born by that date and had survived smallpox, she would have been immune to the disease at the time it hit the Mohawks and would not have been among the dead. Most likely Tekakwitha's mother was about twenty-five at the time of her death.

7. Chauchetiere, *The Life of the Good Catherine*, chap. 6.

8. Chauchetiere, *The Life of the Good Catherine*, chap. 3.

9. Chauchetiere, *The Life of the Good Catherine*, chap. 4.

10. Chauchetiere, *The Life of the Good Catherine*, chap. 4.

11. Ellen H. Walworth, *The Life and Times of Kateri Tekakwitha: The Lily of the Mohawks* (Buffalo: P. Paul, 1998), e-book.

12. Chauchetiere, *The Life of the Good Catherine*, chap. 3.

13. Adriaen Van Der Donck, *A Description of New Netherland*, trans. Diedcrik Willem Goedhuys (Lincoln, Neb.: University of Nebraska Press, 2008), p. 80.

14. Snow, *The Iroquois*, p. 7.

15. *The Jesuit Relations*, vol. 42, pp. 64–67.

16. Alan Greer, *Mohawk Saint: Catherine Tekakwitha and the Jesuits* (New York: Oxford University Press, 2006), pp. 36–37.

17. See information about the Freeman Site in the Appendix.

18. Henri Bechard, S.J., *Kaia'tano:ron Kateri Tekakwitha*, trans. Antoinette Kinlough (Quebec: Kateri Center Kahnawake, 1994), 30.

19. R.G. Thwaites, cd., *The Jesuit Relations and Allied Documents*, vol. 50 (Cleveland : The Burrow Brothers, 1896–1900), pp. 139–141.

20. Bechard, *Kaia'tano:ron Kateri Tekakwitha*, 30.

21. See information about the Fox Farm Site in the Appendix.

Chapter Three

1. Bechard, *Kaia'tano:ron Kateri Tekakwitha*, 34.

2. Chauchetiere, *The Life of the Good Catherine*, chap. 2.

3. Bechard, *Kaia'tano:ron Kateri Tekakwitha*, 38.

4. Bechard, *Kaia'tano:ron Kateri Tekakwitha*, 48.

5. Bechard, *Kaia'tano:ron Kateri Tekakwitha*, 60.

Chapter Four

1. Bechard, *Kaia'tano:ron Kateri Tekakwitha*, 67.

2. Chauchetiere, *The Life of the Good Catherine*, chap. 6.
3. Chauchetiere, *The Life of the Good Catherine*, chap. 7.
4. Chaucheteire, *The Life of the Good Catherine*, chap. 6.
5. Matthew and Margaret Bunson, *Saint Kateri: Lily of the Mohawks* (Huntington, Ind.: Our Sunday Visitor, 2012), 141.
6. Pierre Cholenec, S.J., *The Life of Catherine Tekakwitha, First Iroquois Virgin* (1913), p. 11.

Chapter Five

1. Cholenec, *The Life of Catherine Tekakwitha*, p. 52.
2. Chauchetiere, *The Life of the Good Catherine*, chap. 5.
3. Bechard, KM #2, pp. 4–5. This wampum belt remained in the Church of St. Francis Xavier until 1970 when it was stolen from the current church.
4. Bechard, KM #83, Spring 1970.
5. Bechard, KM #90, Christmas '71.
6. Chauchetiere, *The Life of the Good Catherine*, chap. 13.
7. Bechard, KM #87, Spring 1971.
8. Bechard, *Kaia'tano:ron Kateri Tekakwitha*, 92.
9. Elisabeth Tooker, *Native North American Spirituality of the Eastern Woodlands, Sacred Myths, Dreams, Visions, Speeches, Healing Formulas, Rituals and Ceremonies* (New York: Paulist, 1979), pp. 58–59.
10. Elizabeth A. Smith, *Myths of the Iroquois* (Ontario, Canada: Iroqrafts Ltd., Iroquois Publications, 1989), p. 34.
11. Bechard, *Kaia'tano:ron Kateri Tekakwitha*, 106; Chauchetiere, *The Life of the Good Catherine*, chap. 14.
12. Cholenec, *The Life of Catherine Tekakwitha*, p. 53.
13. Van Der Donck, *A Description of New Netherland*, p. 87.
14. Van Der Donck, *A Description of New Netherland*, p. 56.

15. Chauchetiere, *The Life of the Good Catherine*, chap. 16.

16. Bechard, *Kaia'tano:ron Kateri Tekakwitha*, 114.

17. Bechard, *Kaia'tano:ron Kateri Tekakwitha*, 114.

18. Bechard, *Kaia'tano:ron Kateri Tekakwitha*, 114.

Chapter Six

1. Cholenec, *The Life of Catherine Tekakwitha*, p. 61.

2. Cholenec, *The Life of Catherine Tekakwitha*, p. 57.

3 Bechard, *Kaia'tano:ron Kateri Tekakwitha*, 146.

4. Bechard, *Kaia'tano:ron Kateri Tekakwitha*, 149.

5. Bechard, *Kaia'tano:ron Kateri Tekakwitha*, 116.

6. Bechard, *Kaia'tano:ron Kateri Tekakwitha*, 151.

7. Some traditions say that Kateri said, "Jesus, I love you."

8. Chauchetiere, *The Life of the Good Catherine*, chap. 25.

9. Cholenec, *The Life of Catherine Tekakwitha*, p. 82.

10. Bechard, *Kaia'tano:ron Kateri Tekakwitha*, 153.

11. Chauchetiere, *The Life of the Good Catherine*, chap. 19.

12. Bechard, *Kaia'tano:ron Kateri Tekakwitha*, 154.

13. Bechard, *Kaia'tano:ron Kateri Tekakwitha*, 154.

14. Three years later a violent storm destroyed the chapel. The person who was burned was Stephen Tegananokoa, a Native American martyr, killed at Onandaga. One of Kateri's band was also killed there after being kidnapped by the Iroquois.

15. Bechard, *Kaia'tano:ron Kateri Tekakwitha*, 158.

16. Bechard, KM #91, Spring '72.

17. Greer, p. 152.

Chapter Seven

1. Walworth, preface to *The Life and Times of Kateri*.

2. Prayer from beatification Mass.

3. Veeder Site, Appendix.

4. Bechard, KM #125, Autumn '80.
5. "In Praise of Blessed Kateri at Time of Beatification," Catholic Information Network, September 1, 1996, http://www.kateri-tekakwitha.org/kateri/pope.htm.

Chapter Eight

1. Address of His Holiness John Paul II, September 14, 1987. Emphasis in original.
2. Christopher Vecsey, *The Paths of Kateri's Kin* (Notre Dame, Ind.: University of Notre Dame Press, 1997), pp. 107–108.
3. *Ecclesia in America*, p. 233.
4. *Ecclesia in America*, pp. 213–214.
5. 1992: A Time for Remembering, Reconciling, and Recommitting Ourselves as a People, Statement of the National Conference of Catholic Bishops on Native Americans, November 1991, p. 2.
6. June 11, 2008 Apology.
7. April 17, 2008 Apology.
8. "Native American Catholics at the Millennium," p. 4.
9. "Native American Catholics at the Millennium," p. 6.

Chapter Nine

1. "Letter of the Holy Father John Paul II to Cardinal Fiorenzo Angelini for the 50th Anniversary of the Benedictine Sisters of Reparation of the Holy Face," September 27, 2000, http://www.vatican.va/holy_father/john_paul_ii/letters/2000/documents/hf_jp-ii_let_20001021_riparatrici_en.html.

Bibliography

Aufderheide, Arthur C., Conrado Rodriguez-Martin, and Odin Langsjoen. *The Cambridge Encyclopedia of Human Paleopathology.* Cambridge, U.K.: Cambridge University Press, 1998.

Bechard, S.J., Henri. *Kaia'tano:ron Kateri Tekakwitha.* Translated by Antoinette Kinlough. Quebec: Kateri Center Kahnawake, 1994.

Bonaparte, Darren. *A Lily Among Thorns: The Mohawk Repatriation of Kateri Tekahkwitha.* The Mohawk Territory of Akwesasne: The Wampum Chronicles, 2009.

Bunson, Matthew and Margaret. *Saint Kateri: Lily of the Mohawks.* Huntington, Ind.: Our Sunday Visitor, 2012.

Burke, Jr., Thomas E. *Mohawk Frontier: The Dutch Community of Schenectady, New York, 1661–1710.* 2nd ed. Albany, N.Y.: State University of New York Press, 1991.

Chauchetiere, Claude, S.J. *The Life of the Good Catherine Tekakwitha.* (n.p.: 1695).

Cholenec, Pierre, S.J. *The Life of Catherine Tekakwitha, First Iroquois Virgin.* (n.p.: 1913).

The Jesuit Relations and Allied Documents.

Porter, Tom. *Clanology, Clan System of the Iroquois.* Cornwall, Ontario: Native American Travelling College, 1993.

Smith, Elizabeth A. *Myths of the Iroquois.* Ontario, Canada: Iroqrafts Ltd., Iroquois Publications, 1989.

Snow, Dean R. *Mohawk Valley Archaeology: The Sites.* Albany, N.Y.: The Institute for Archaeological Studies, University at Albany, SUNY, 1995.

————. *Mohawk Valley Archaeology: The Collections.* University Park, Penn.: Matson Museum of Anthropology, Pennsylvania State University, 1995.

————. *The Iroquois.* Malden, Mass.: Blackwell, 1994.

Tooker, Elisabeth. *Native North American Spirituality of the Eastern Woodlands, Sacred Myths, Dreams, Visions, Speeches, Healing Formulas, Rituals and Ceremonies.* New York: Paulist, 1979.

Van der Donck, Adriaen. *A Description of New Netherland.* Translated by Diederik Willem Goedhuys. Lincoln, Neb.: University of Nebraska Press, 2008.

Vecsey, Christopher. *The Paths of Kateri's Kin.* Notre Dame, Ind.: University of Notre Dame Press, 1997.

Waldman, Carl. *Encyclopedia of Native American Tribes.* 3rd ed. New York: Checkmark, 2006.

Walworth, Ellen H. *The Life and Times of Kateri Tekakwitha: The Lily of the Mohawks.* Buffalo, N.Y.: P. Paul, 1998.

PRAYER
for
HEALING

ABOUT THE AUTHOR

Emily Cavins is the coeditor of *Amazing Grace for Mothers* and the developer of the Great Adventure Kids Bible study materials, a system for teaching children the plan of salvation history. Emily and her husband, Jeff, have been married for over thirty years and are the parents of three daughters.